ISBN 978-1-331-23833-1
PIBN 10162718

English
Français
Deutsche
Italiano
Español
Português

www.forgottenbooks.com

Mythology Photography **Fiction**
Fishing Christianity **Art** Cooking
Essays Buddhism Freemasonry
Medicine **Biology** Music **Ancient
Egypt** Evolution Carpentry Physics
Dance Geology **Mathematics** Fitness
Shakespeare **Folklore** Yoga Marketing
Confidence Immortality Biographies
Poetry **Psychology** Witchcraft
Electronics Chemistry History **Law**
Accounting **Philosophy** Anthropology
Alchemy Drama Quantum Mechanics
Atheism Sexual Health **Ancient History**
Entrepreneurship Languages Sport
Paleontology Needlework Islam
Metaphysics Investment Archaeology
Parenting Statistics Criminology
Motivational

Addison Alexander,

Princeton,

April 21, 1855.

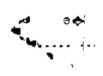

HINTS

FOR

AN IMPROVED TRANSLATION

OF THE

NEW TESTAMENT.

BY THE

REV. JAMES SCHOLEFIELD, A.M.

REGIUS PROFESSOR OF GREEK IN THE UNIVERSITY OF CAMBRIDGE,
AND CANON OF ELY.

THIRD EDITION,
WITH THE APPENDIX INCORPORATED.

LONDON:
JOHN W. PARKER, WEST STRAND.
M.DCCC.L.

Cambridge:
Printed at the University Press.

PREFACE

TO THE FIRST EDITION.

IT is possible that this little work may be met with an objection *in limine,* quite independent of the manner in which it is executed,—viz. that to call the public attention to the consideration of any supposed improvements in the authorised version of our Bibles is needlessly to unsettle men's minds, and shake their confidence in a book which is familiarised with their daily occupations and habits of thinking, and towards which therefore it is desirable that they should entertain no other feelings than those of a reposing conviction of its practical perfection.

I do not under-rate this objection. But my answer to it is, that in proportion to the importance of having the sacred text settled is the importance also of having it settled on a true and safe foundation. And there may probably be readers among the ordinary ranks of those who go every day to *draw water out of* these *wells of salvation,* who may sometimes encounter a degree of perplexity in weighing and comparing together some of the more difficult passages as they stand in our translation. And there may possibly also be some among the preachers of the word, who, as they meditate upon it in preparing to divide it to others, may find it difficult to reconcile the associations of thought, which have grown up with them from their infancy, with the more matured views which open upon their minds in carrying their inquiries higher, up to the fountain of the sacred original. And with regard to both these classes it is important to bear in mind this distinction, that whatever obscurity is found in God's word arising from the mysterious nature of its sub-lime revelations, is a fit exercise for patience and humility and child-like prayer for the teaching of that Holy Spirit by whose inspiration it was given; but if it possess any adventitious difficulty, resulting from a defective trans-lation, then it is at the same time an act of charity and of duty to clear away that difficulty as much as possible, and present it to the English reader with the greatest attain-able advantage.

Nor let it for a moment be supposed, that such an attempt implies a shadow of reproach upon the original Translators. For myself, I would rather blot out from the catalogue of my country's worthies the names of Bacon and Newton, than those of the venerable men, who were raised up by the providence of God, and endowed by his Spirit, to achieve for England her greatest blessing in the authorised translation of the Scriptures. If in the following pages, the professed object of which is to express opinions on minor points differing from theirs, I have dropped any expressions in speaking of them which even an unkind criticism can charge with any thing like flippancy or a want of the most grateful veneration for them, I would gladly, if it were possible, wash out with my tears the obnoxious passages, and rather leave their glorious work soiled with its few human blemishes, than attempt to beautify it at the expense of their well-earned renown. But I have thought that, in entire consistency with the honest sincerity of this feeling, something might be attempted towards carrying a little nearer to perfection a work which is already so near to it.

If I succeed, however, in conciliating the Reader towards the undertaking of such a project at all, there will be many things in the execution of it, which may seem perhaps less entitled to his indulgence. Some of the annotations may appear not to be original enough, and others to be too original; I mean, too far removed from received modes of explaining the difficulties of this holy Book. Some may be thought not sufficiently important to warrant the attempt at disturbing what is already established in possession of the text: on some occasions I may have expressed an opinion without bringing argument or authority enough to support it, and on others I may have been too diffuse.—I will not detain the reader with any lengthened explanations on these and other points, but will merely state, that the corrections here proposed are in general the result of my own study of the sacred volume, though I have on many occasions been led to examine what others had written on a difficult passage, and perhaps partially to adopt it, even without express acknowledgment; that I have never proposed a translation for the sake of its novelty, but from an honest conviction of its truth, that conviction varying in its strength according to the terms in which it is expressed; that while some of the following remarks are confessedly

not important enough to form an occasion for bringing
forward the general subject, it may not be unseasonable
to have inserted them among the rest, in the hope that
they may not be without their use to younger students;
and finally, that this little book is after all only elementary,
designed to call the attention of others to an important
subject, and to scatter "seeds of thought" which may be
afterwards matured into ripe results of practical benefit.

If ever in this inquiring age this subject were taken in
hand with a view to accomplishing that for which the
present pages contain "Hints," justice, not only to King
James's Translators, but to the great mass of our popu-
lation, who have nothing but the English Bible for the
DAILY BREAD of their souls, would require that the alterations made in the text should be as few as possible,
and that none should be made at all but what after
full deliberation should be considered quite necessary.
There is one point which would seem important to
attend to, which indeed it may appear surprising that
our Translators attended to so little,—uniformity; the
uniform rendering of the same Greek word, as far as
might be, by the same English word.   The want of this
is in a measure to be accounted for by different parts
being executed by different Translators; but this will
not account for it in the same book and the same
chapter.   See, for example, on Romans v.*

---

* This objection however is partly anticipated by our Translators at the close of their interesting address to the Reader.

With regard to the Marginal Readings of our Bibles, —a most important kind of commentary, when no other is within reach,—the Reader is to be reminded, that they are not all inserted by the Translators, but many are of a much more recent date, and consequently do not possess the same authority: few of them, however, can be considered other than useful.

It is scarcely necessary to observe, that the chief difficulties of the New Testament will be found in the Epistles: the Reader may consequently expect, in going through the Gospels, to find comparatively few remarks in the following pages, and those perhaps not of great importance. Having in the beginning noticed the translation of the Greek Article in several passages, in which I could of course do little else than follow Bishop Middleton, I have afterwards declined to introduce what would have been mere repetition.

The reader will easily discover what is the plan of this publication, viz. first to print in the Italic character the authorised version of the passages to be remarked upon; then the original Greek; and then the proposed correction, followed by remarks. Those words which are printed in Italics in our Bibles, as not being in the original, are here, in the quotations from the Bible, printed in the ordinary character, being so distinguished from the character in which the passage itself is printed.

CAMBRIDGE,
Jan. 2, 1832.

PREFACE

TO THE SECOND EDITION.

THE title of this publication has, not unnaturally, led to the inquiry, whether I was really desirous that a new translation of the Greek Testament should be undertaken: to which my reply has uniformly been in the negative. The real design of it was rather to assist towards the understanding of the old translation, than to supersede it by a new one; to furnish a kind of running commentary, for clearing up difficulties as they arose, by presenting the different passages in an English form more accurately corresponding to the original. In pursuance of this object I have mixed up with the new readings explanatory remarks, one leading principle of which is to trace accurately the connexion of the writer's thoughts; from not perceiving which in some instances our Translators seem to have missed the sense of the original, and from neglecting which in others they have failed to exhibit it to the mere English reader. These remarks have sometimes run out to a considerable length, particularly in the additional notes supplied in this edition. In some cases also additions have been made, for the sake of greater perspicuity, to the notes contained in the former edition. All the additions thus made, except where they were too unimportant to deserve notice, are included between brackets. An Index is also added for the convenience of reference.

September, 1836.

PREFACE

TO THE THIRD EDITION.

In sending forth a new and enlarged edition of these remarks on particular passages, it may not be without its use to younger students of the sacred volume, if I prefix a few observations on some general points, by attending to which the sense of the writers may frequently be much cleared and simplified.

1. Not a few passages in our Translation are obscured by a want of strict attention to the *tenses* of the original, and, in consequence, the improper insertion or omission of the auxiliary verb *have*. The distinction between the aorist and perfect tenses of the Greek is clearly marked, and in general it is accurately observed in the New Testament. And though the difference of idiom between the two languages may occasionally require a deviation from the strict rule of grammar, such deviations appear to be carelessly and causelessly admitted in our authorised version in many instances to the serious disturbance of the sense.

The following are a few examples of the improper *insertion* of *have*, by which the sense of the original is more or less interfered with. 1 Cor. xi. 23. 'For I *have received* ($\pi\alpha\rho\dot{\epsilon}\lambda\alpha\beta o\nu$) of the Lord that which also I delivered ($\pi\alpha\rho\dot{\epsilon}\delta\omega\kappa\alpha$) unto you.' Here the two verbs are both in the aorist tense, and it is obvious that both should be rendered in the same form: *I received,*

i. e. at a certain definite time, to which reference is made
by the tense employed. Again, 2 Pet. i. 14. 'Even
as our Lord Jesus Christ *hath shewed* me,' ἐδήλωσε—
shewed me; viz. on the memorable occasion mentioned
John xxi. 18. This is a less faulty example; but one
much worse occurs in ver. 16 of the same chapter: 'For
we *have not followed* (ἐξακολουθήσαντες) cunningly devised fables, when we made known (ἐγνωρίσαμεν) unto
you the power and coming of our Lord Jesus Christ,
but *were* (γενηθέντες) eye-witnesses of his majesty.' The
confusion introduced into this verse requires more than
one correction. In 2 Cor. vii. 8, ἐλύπησεν is *made you
sorry*, not, *hath made*, any more than ἐλύπησα at the
beginning of the verse is, *I have made*: in 1 Thess. iv.
1. παρελάβετε, *ye received;* 2 Tim. i. 13. and ii. 2,
ἤκουσας, *thou heardest;* and 1 Pet. i. 10, ἐξεζήτησαν,
inquired—without *have.*

In a few instances the same auxiliary is improperly
omitted: John xv. 18, μεμίσηκεν, and 24, πεποίηκεν.
Another passage in the same Gospel, chap. vi. 32, is
entitled to deeper consideration: 'Moses hath not given
(δέδωκεν) you the bread from heaven; but my Father
giveth, is (now) giving, you the true bread from heaven.'
Compare also γέγονεν in Matth. xxvi. 56.

2. The next observation has reference to the Greek
Article. The liberties taken by our Translators with this
important element of biblical criticism constitute perhaps
the greatest blot in their admirable work. Numerous
instances are pointed out in the following notes: one or
two will suffice here to illustrate the general remark.

Article *omitted,* or the indefinite substituted for the definite. Matth. viii. 23. τὸ πλοῖον, *a ship.* Cf. ver. 18. Luke vii. 5. τὴν συναγωγὴν, a synagogue. Acts xxiv. 23. τῷ ἑκατοντάρχῃ, *a centurion.* Ephes. ii. 18. τὴν προσαγωγὴν, *an access.* Acts xxiii. 27. σὺν τῷ στρατεύματι, *with an army.* It should be, *with the soldiers,* as in ver. 10; or, *with the soldiery,* preserving the abstract form of the original.

Inserted. Luke iii. 14. στρατευόμενοι, *the soldiers.* 2 Pet. i. 21. προφητεία, *the prophecy.*

Mistranslated. John i. 8. τὸ φῶς, *that light.* vi. 48. ὁ ἄρτος, *that bread.* Acts xix. 9. τὴν ὁδὸν, *that way.* 2 Corinth. v. 1. τοῦ σκήνους, *of this tabernacle.* See on Matth. xv. 12.

3. The student of the New Testament will sometimes find the *Prepositions* a source of considerable difficulty or uncertainty. This arises perhaps from the familiarity of the writers with the Hebrew language, in which the prepositions are much fewer than in the Greek: but whatever be the cause, it is undoubtedly true in fact, that not only they are frequently translated in our version in an unusual manner, but the sense of the original evidently requires such deviation from customary usage. Some care then is necessary to determine the sense of prepositions in particular passages. It is not meant that our Translators are frequently in error in this respect; but the consideration of a few examples may assist to a right understanding of the principle.

The preposition ἐν seems to be used with great latitude by the inspired writers, but is sometimes also incorrectly rendered in our translation. Luke xxiii. 42, ἐν τῇ βασιλείᾳ σου, into *thy kingdom*, is any thing but an improvement on the literal rendering, *in*. Gal. ii. 20, ἐν πίστει, by *the faith*, is doubtful: Ephes. iv. 32, ἐν Χριστῷ, *for Christ's sake*, is unnecessary. In 1 Corinth. i. 4, 5, ἐν Χριστῷ Ἰησοῦ, ἐν αὐτῷ, the literal rendering is better, *in Christ Jesus, in him;* on the other hand, in ver. 6, ἐβεβαιώθη ἐν ὑμῖν should be *among you*. In 2 Pet. i. 5—7, ἐπιχορηγήσατε ἐν τῇ πίστει, &c., *add* to *your faith*, appears to be correct.

The use of διὰ is frequently anomalous. (See on Matth. xv. 3, 6.) In some cases there is obscurity arising not from mistranslation, but from its being rendered *by* in the sense of *through*, as in Ephes. iii. 10. In 2 Tim. ii. 2, διὰ πολλῶν μαρτύρων, among *many witnesses*, is a questionable rendering: the marginal *by* is perhaps preferable. On similar grounds 1 Thess. iv. 14, τοὺς κοιμηθέντας διὰ τοῦ Ἰησοῦ, *in Jesus*, is not without its difficulty. The Vulgate has, *per Jesum*. Beza, who translates *in Jesu*, remarks: *id est, ἐν τῷ Ἰησοῦ,... ut διὰ pro ἐν ponatur, sicut diximus Rom. iv. 11, et ut vertit hoc loco Syrus interpres.* In 2 Corinth. iii. 11, διὰ δόξης and ἐν δόξῃ *appear* to be used promiscuously.—The difference between διὰ and ὑπὸ, as both represented by the English preposition *by*, must be carefully observed. Ex. gr. in Hebr. ii. 2, δι' ἀγγέλων λαληθεὶς, *spoken by angels*, conveys to an English reader the idea that angels were the speakers who pronounced the law, just as if it had been ὑπ' ἀγγέλων, whereas the meaning of διὰ is *through, through the intervention* or *ministry of*, as subordinate agents. So Galat. iii. 19, διαταγεὶς δι᾽ ἀγγέλων, *ordained by angels,* i. e. *through.* (Compare Acts vii. 53, εἰς διαταγὰς ἀγγέλων, *by the disposition* of angels.) And both in John i. 3, πάντα δι᾽ αὐτοῦ ἐγένετο, and Hebr. ii. 3, ἀρχὴν λαβοῦσα λαλεῖσθαι διὰ τοῦ Κυρίου, the preposition may be understood in its strict and proper sense without the slightest disparagement of the divine glory of the Saviour, who is represented as acting ministerially in the respective economies of creation and redemption. On the other hand, in 1 Corinth. i. 9, πιστὸς ὁ Θεὸς, δι᾽ οὖ ἐκλήθητε, it seems impossible to understand διὰ otherwise than as used for ὑπό. A very few copies indeed read ὑπό, and Beza, who translates *per quem,* remarks: "Id est, ὑφ᾽ οὖ, *a quo,* ut habet etiam Claromontanus codex. Est enim *promiscuus* harum præpositionum usus." The last assertion is too lax; but the remark grounded upon it is important: "Ut plane inepti sint qui istis syllabarum aucupiis conantur homines imperitos irretire," &c.

It should likewise be borne in mind, that the sense of ὑπό, which we commonly express by the preposition *by,* was more generally rendered by our Translators by *of;* as Matth. xiv. 8, *instructed* of *her mother,* ὑπὸ τῆς μητρός. Another ambiguity also in the English preposition *of* is worth noticing: in John iii. 31, *he that is of the earth is earthly, and speaketh of the earth,* the original is ἐκ τῆς γῆς,—not *concerning,* but *from.*

Several instances of anomaly or peculiarity in the use of εἰς are pointed out in the following notes. See

on Matth. xiii. 9; Rom. i. 17; Gal. iii. 17, &c.
Again, as in Luke xxiii. 42, ἐν βασιλείᾳ is rendered
into, so in Matth. xxviii. 19, εἰς τὸ ὄνομα is translated
in the name. Compare 1 Corinth. x. 2. In 1 Pet. i.
11, the remarkable form, τὰ εἰς Χριστὸν παθήματα,
is perhaps rightly rendered *the sufferings of Christ.*
Compare with it Ephes. i. 15, τὴν καθ' ὑμᾶς πίστιν,
your faith: and there is something not very unlike it in
the expression of Demosthenes, F. L. 365, 6, τοῦ περὶ
Φωκέας ὀλέθρου.

A few instances occur in the New Testament of
a peculiar class of Greek expressions, which are generally rendered with strict accuracy in our version:
John xv. 24, ἁμαρτίαν οὐκ εἶχον, for οὐκ ἂν εἶχον,
they had not had sin; Rom. ix. 3, ηὐχόμην γὰρ, *for 1
could wish**. It deserves to be considered whether
Galat. iv. 20, ἤθελον δὲ παρεῖναι, should not be brought
under the same class: *but I* could wish *to be present.*

Καὶ τανῦν παρατίθεμαι ὑμᾶς, ἀδελφοὶ, τῷ Θεῷ καὶ
ΤΩͺ ΛΟΓΩͺ ΤΗΣ ΧΑΡΙΤΟΣ ΑΥΤΟΥ, τῷ δυναμένῳ
ἐποικοδομῆσαι καὶ δοῦναι ὑμῖν κληρονομίαν ἐν τοῖς
ἡγιασμένοις πᾶσιν. Act. xx. 32.

---

* Aristoph. Ran. 865. ἐβουλόμην μὲν οὐκ ἐρίζειν ἐνθάδε. *I could
wish.*

October, 1850.

HINTS

FOR AN IMPROVED TRANSLATION OF THE NEW TESTAMENT.

ST. MATTHEW.

CHAP. iii. 16. *Out of the water.* ἀπὸ τοῦ ὕδατος. 'From the water.'

iv. 21. *In a ship.* ἐν τῷ πλοίῳ. 'In the ship.' This is the first passage which claims particular notice with reference to the important subject of the Greek Article, which our Translators have in many instances too hastily neglected, where the reason of its insertion was not immediately obvious. As this subject has been so fully discussed by the late Bishop Middleton in his learned work, I shall not in general trouble the reader with any remark on his general principle, but content myself with correcting the translation of passages in which that principle is violated, except in cases where it appears to me that something new may be advanced to throw light on its application. Above, in v. 5, the translation may be corrected, *the* pinnacle.

On the present verse Bishop Middleton remarks, that the words may mean, *in* their *boat;* but I think it sufficient to give the exact literal rendering as above, because the expression, *in the ship with their father,* would evidently mean in their father's ship.

v. i. *Into a mountain.* εἰς τὸ ὄρος. 'Into the mountain.' Bishop Middleton and others understand this of the *mountain-district,* with which I confess myself not entirely satisfied: but though there is certainly some difficulty with regard to the Article in this and a few other instances, it is neither such nor so great as to shake the stability of a principle resting upon usage as nearly universal as possible.

Ib. 15. *A bushel, a candlestick.* τὸν μόδιον, τὴν λυχνίαν. 'The bushel, the candlestick.' Here also Bishop Middleton's note may be referred to.

Ib. 32. *Shall marry her that is divorced.* ἀπολελυμένην γαμήσῃ. 'Shall marry *her* after she is divorced.'

vii. 4. *A beam.* ἡ δοκός. 'The beam'—that mentioned in the preceding verse.

Ib. 24, 25. *Upon a rock.* ἐπὶ τὴν πέτραν. 'Upon the rock.' The use of the Article appears very similar to that noticed on v. 1; to which it may be added, that the word πέτρα here has a peculiar distinctness as opposed to the ἄμμος which follows.

viii. 32. *Down a steep place.* κατὰ τοῦ κρημνοῦ. 'Down the precipice, or rock.'

ix. 1. *Into a ship.* εἰς τὸ πλοῖον. 'Into the ship.' But what ship? That mentioned Mark iii. 9, as pointed out by Bishop Middleton, who quotes a good note of Gilbert Wakefield on Matt. xiii. 2.

Ib. 10. *In the house.* ἐν τῇ οἰκίᾳ. 'In his house'—viz. Matthew's, who, as St Luke informs us (v. 29), *made him a great feast in his own house.* This use of the Article, in the sense of a *possessive pronoun,* is referred to by Bishop Middleton in Part I. Chap. III. Sect. 1. § 4, and is so common that it can hardly be considered elliptical, though, strictly speaking, αὐτοῦ is understood after οἰκίᾳ. I have not therefore printed 'his' in Italics.*

Ib. 17. *Old bottles.* ἀσκοὺς παλαιούς. 'Old leathern bottles.' Though in the translation of such a book as the Bible a general expression is far better than one *needlessly* minute, yet in the present instance it is obvious that the passage to an English reader loses all its meaning in the common translation, being so directly contradictory to the fact as he will understand it.—The nature of the bottles being defined on the first mention, the epithet (*leathern*) need not be repeated in the three examples of the word's repetition.

x. 10. *Nor yet staves.* μηδὲ ῥάβδον. 'Nor yet a staff.'

Ib. 11. *Town.* κώμην. 'Village.' So translated ix. 35, and elsewhere; and more suitable here from its opposition to *city.*

Ib. 12. *An house.* τὴν οἰκίαν. 'The house'—viz. of the person referred to in the preceding verse as *worthy* to entertain them.

Ib. 18. *For a testimony against them and the Gentiles.*

[* On this point, however, it is judiciously observed by the Dean of Peterborough, (now Bishop of Ely—*Text of the English Bible considered,* p. 25,) that there is a reason why the possessive pronoun should in these cases be printed in Italics, viz. to distinguish them from those in which the original has the corresponding pronoun inserted—as in the passage above referred to, St Matthew has ἐν τῇ οἰκίᾳ, St Luke ἐν τῇ οἰκίᾳ αὐτοῦ.]

εἰς μαρτύριον αὐτοῖς καὶ τοῖς ἔθνεσιν. 'For a testimony to them and the Gentiles.' This is all that the original expresses, and it determines nothing as to the character of the testimony. So in the corresponding passage, Mark xiii. 9. Nor is the sense *expressed* different in Mark vi. 11, though there the meaning of the expression is determined by the parallel passage in Luke ix. 5, εἰς μαρτύριον ἐπ' αὐτούς. But this is a question of interpretation, not of translation.

Ib. 23. *Another.* τὴν ἄλλην. 'The other,' or 'the next.'

Ib. 30. *But the very hairs of your head are all numbered.* ὑμῶν δὲ καὶ αἱ τρίχες τῆς κεφαλῆς πᾶσαι ἠριθμημέναι εἰσί. 'But *as to you*, even the hairs of your head are all numbered.' In the original there is a marked emphasis in the position of ὑμῶν, as opposed to στρουθία in the preceding verse. In our translation this emphasis is lost. I cannot suggest a better way of expressing it than that offered above.

xi. 14. *This is.* αὐτός ἐστιν. 'He is'—viz. John, mentioned just before.

xii. 43. *When.* Ὅταν δέ. 'But when.' The aggravated sin of the Jews in rejecting Christ having been set forth in the preceding verses, this and the two following verses are added to explain the awful process by which they had been brought into that hardened state. The conjunction, which our Translators have passed over, is of great use for marking the connexion.

xiii. 2. *A ship.* τὸ πλοῖον. 'The ship.' See on ix. 1.

Ib. 19. *This is he which received seed by the way-side.*
οὗτός ἐστιν ὁ παρὰ τὴν ὁδὸν σπαρείς. 'This is that which
was sown by the way-side.' Our Translators have introduced great confusion by a want of uniformity in their
version of this parable in the three Evangelists. In St.
Matthew they uniformly (vv. 19, 20, 22, 23) render the
passive participle σπαρείς by the idea of *receiving seed*, as
if it applied to the field instead of the seed. But as
σπαρείς properly signifies *sown*, not *receiving seed;* so our
Lord in his own interpretation of the parable explains
the seed sown of those who by the word are sown or
planted in the church: just as in the next parable he
says, v. 38, *The good seed are the children of the kingdom.*
It must be confessed indeed, that there is some little
confusion in the use of the metaphor; but then a translation should not make the confusion greater than it is
in the original. The confusion consists in the *seed* being
interpreted primarily of *the word of God*, and secondarily
of the *children*, either of the kingdom of God or of the
wicked one. Mark says, iv. 14, *The sower soweth the word:*
Luke, viii. 11, *The seed is the word of God.* But when our
Lord goes on to distribute the primary and general idea
into its parts in reference to the results, this can only be
done by marking the distinction in the characters produced. And these different results, again, are owing not
to any difference in the seed, which is the same in all,
viz. *the word of God;* but to the difference of the grounds
in which it is sown. This is clearly expressed in the
translation of Mark iv. 16, 18, 20, *These are they which are.*

sown on stony ground, &c. &c.—whereas in v. 15 it is expressed in the other form, *These are they by the way-side, where* THE WORD *is sown, but,* &c.—If any prefer to render in Matthew as in Mark, *This is* HE *which was sown by the way-side,* there can be no objection to it.

Ib. 21. *By and by.* εὐθύς. 'Immediately.'

Ib. 22. *And he becometh unfruitful.* καὶ ἄκαρπος γίνεται. 'And it becometh unfruitful.'

Ib. 27. *Tares.* τὰ ζιζάνια. 'The tares,' as it is rightly rendered in v. 26.

Ib. 42. *A furnace.* τὴν κάμινον. 'The furnace.'

xiv. 22. *A ship.* τὸ πλοῖον. 'The ship.' So, next v. τὸ ὄρος, 'the mountain,' as in v. 1. Perhaps it may signify the *nearest mountain,* as if taking it for granted that there was one not far off.

xv. 1. *Scribes and Pharisees which were of Jerusalem.* Οἱ ἀπὸ Ἱεροσολύμων γραμματεῖς καὶ Φαρισαῖοι. 'The Scribes and Pharisees from Jerusalem'—not meaning of course all of them, but a large body of them.

Ib. 3, 6. *By your tradition.* διὰ τὴν παράδοσιν ὑμῶν. 'Because of your tradition.' The difference in this instance is not great; but so important in many other passages is the distinction between the sense of διὰ with a genitive and with an accusative, that it is worth while to shew that the two senses are never confounded. (Doubtless Rev. xii. 11, ἐνίκησαν αὐτὸν διὰ τὸ αἷμα τοῦ ἀρνίου καὶ διὰ τὸν λόγον τῆς μαρτυρίας αὐτῶν, may be adduced as an exception; but the peculiar style of that book sufficiently accounts for it. There occurs another example of a similar irregularity, but it is in the same writer, John vi. 57: καθὼς ἀπέστειλέ με ὁ ζῶν πατὴρ, κἀγὼ ζῶ διὰ τὸν πατέρα· καὶ ὁ τρώγων με, κἀκεῖνος ζήσεται δι' ἐμέ. In both these passages however the strict sense of διὰ, *because of*, *may be* preserved; and in that case they may be compared with Rom. viii. 11, where the various reading is especially to be noticed.) The statement here is, not that they *transgressed the commandment of God* by making or delivering such a tradition, but that they set aside the one *from a regard to* the other: or, as it is unambiguously expressed in Mark vii. 9, ἵνα τὴν παράδοσιν ὑμῶν τηρήσητε.

Ib. 12. *This saying.* τὸν λόγον. 'Thy saying.' See on ix. 10. Our Translators appear to me to have frequently erred in rendering the Article by the pronoun *this* or *that*. In no case can it be accurately rendered so; though there are instances in which the licence may be admitted for the sake of perspicuity.

Ib. 22. *The same coasts.* τῶν ὁρίων ἐκείνων. 'Those coasts.'

Ib. 27. *Truth, Lord; yet the dogs*—ναὶ, Κύριε· καὶ γὰρ τὰ κυνάρια—'Yea, Lord; for the dogs'—The words in St Mark (vii. 28) are the same as here; and there seems no sufficient reason why καὶ γὰρ should be strained to a sense very unusual at the least, though Romans v. 7 may *seem* to justify it. But I consider ναὶ here to be a form of *imploring*, rather than of assenting; and so the words which follow will contain the reason why her suit should be regarded.

xvii. 24, 27. *Tribute, a piece of money.* τὰ δίδραχμα, στατῆρα. It may be worth a consideration whether the words might not be rendered, 'the half-shekel, a shekel.' Our Translators have here carried to a great length the principle of generalization which I have commended above, on ix. 17, and I am not prepared to say that they have not done wisely: but whether the more literal translation be adopted or not, in either case an explanation is necessary to make the passage intelligible to the unlearned reader.

xx. 11. *The good man of the house.* τοῦ οἰκοδεσπότου. 'The householder.' So translated v. 1, in the introduction of the parable; and the variation is not only needless, but has a quaintness in it not calculated to recommend it.

Ib. 21. *Grant.* εἰπέ. 'Command.'

Ib. 23. *But it shall be given to them for whom*—ἀλλ' οἷς. 'Except *to those* for whom'—By foisting in the supernumerary words we make the passage contain a doctrine directly contrary to other places of Scripture: ex. gr. John xvii. 2. Revelation iii. 21. Precisely the same expression, ἀλλ' οἷς, occurs above in chap. xix. 11, where it is properly translated *save*. So also in 2 Corinth. ii. 5, ἀλλ' ἀπὸ μέρους. But in this passage the various readings must be considered.

Ib. 31. *Rebuked them because*—ἐπετίμησεν αὐτοῖς ἵνα— 'Charged them that'—The same words are so translated in St Mark's narrative of the same incident, x. 48. See also Luke xviii. 39, where a middle course is adopted in the translation; and compare the use of ἐπιτιμήσας in Luke ix. 21.

xxiii. 6. *The uppermost rooms.* τὴν πρωτοκλισίαν. 'The chief places.' The word *rooms* conveys an erroneous idea to the ordinary reader.

xxiv. 32. *Is yet tender.* ἤδη ... γένηται ἀπαλός. 'Is now become tender.'

xxvi. 15. *They covenanted with him for—*ἔστησαν αὐτῷ. 'They weighed to him.' This translation seems to be justly preferred by many learned men, not only on account of its being more literal, but because the words appear to be a designed quotation of the Septuagint translation of Zech. xi. 12, ἔστησαν τὸν μισθόν μου τριά-κοντα ἀργυροῦς· where our Translators properly render the original word, *they weighed.* The expressions in Mark and Luke are quite different.

Ib. 28. *Of the new testament.* τὸ τῆς καινῆς διαθήκης. 'The *blood* of the new covenant.' The difficult question about the word διαθήκη will be entered upon at Hebr. ix. 15.

Ib. 33. *Peter answered and said.* ἀποκριθεὶς δὲ ὁ Πέτρος εἶπεν. 'But Peter answered and said.' The omission of the copula here by our Translators may appear very unimportant; and in this instance, so it is: but they have taken the same liberty in other passages, where it is by no means an indifferent matter; and it is well there-fore to mark the practice where there is no ulterior use to be made of it. See chap. vii. 15, xii. 43.

Ib. 54. *But how then.* πῶς οὖν. '*But* how then.'

Ib. 56. *But all this was done, that the scriptures of the prophets might be fulfilled.* Τοῦτο δὲ ὅλον γέγονεν, ἵνα πληρωθῶσιν αἱ γραφαὶ τῶν προφητῶν. 'But all this is done, that the scriptures of the prophets may be fulfilled.' This is the more literal translation; and so the passage is to be considered, not as the inspired comment of the writer, but as the conclusion of the Saviour's address. Compare Mark xiv. 49, where instead of rendering, *the scriptures must be fulfilled,* we must supply from Matthew, this is done *that the scriptures may be fulfilled.* See on the passage. Compare also Luke xxii. 53.

Ib. 61. *In three days.* διὰ τριῶν ἡμερῶν. 'After three days.' More literal to the original, and more exact to the sense of the passage.

xxvii. 23. *Why? what*—(So it stands in some editions.) τί γὰρ—'Why, what'—Thus pointed, the translation is not only correct, but happy and elegant.

Ib. 27. *The whole band* of soldiers. ὅλην τὴν σπεῖραν. 'Their whole company.' For the translation *their* see on ix. 10. In the common version the insertion of the words *of soldiers* makes an inelegant and harsh repetition, which may easily be avoided either by the above method, or by supplying 'the whole band of them.'

ST. MARK.

CHAP. i. 6. *A girdle of a skin.* ζώνην δερματίνην. 'A leathern girdle.' There is no objection to the received translation here; except that the same words are rendered in Matthew iii. 4 as I have here proposed; and it is obviously desirable in the translation of a book like the N. T. to retain, as nearly as possible, the identity of expression when it is retained in the original.

ii. 18. *Used to fast.* ἦσαν ... νηστεύοντες. 'Were fasting.' Happened at that time to be keeping one of their many fasts (Luke v. 33), and were either offended or perplexed at seeing the disciples of Christ neglecting it.

iii. 3. *The withered hand.* ἐξηραμμένην — τὴν χεῖρα. 'His hand withered.' This is more correct, and so it would be also in the first verse; but the variation is not important in either case.

Ib. 13. See on Matt. v. 1.

iv. 1. *A ship.* τὸ πλοῖον. 'The ship.' See on Matt. ix. 1.

Ib. 21. *A candle, a bushel, a bed, a candlestick.* ὁ λύχνος, etc. Matt. v. 15.

Ib. 37. *Was now full.* ἤδη γεμίζεσθαι. 'Was now filling.'

v. 38. *And them that wept.* κλαίοντας. 'Persons weeping.' Some copies however insert καὶ before κλαίοντας: if it be considered better to retain it with our Translators, *and* may be inserted before *persons.*

Ib. 40. *And they laughed him to scorn.* καὶ κατεγέλων αὐτοῦ. 'And they laughed at him.' There seems nothing in the original to warrant the harsh language of our translation. So Matt. ix. 24. Luke viii. 53.

vi. 21. *And when a convenient day was come, that*— καὶ γενομένης ἡμέρας εὐκαίρου, ὅτε—'And a convenient day being come, when'—

Ib. 56. *In the streets.* ἐν ταῖς ἀγοραῖς. 'In the market-places.' πλατείαις, the original of *streets*, is the reading of but few copies.

vii. 28. See on Matt. xv. 27.

viii. 36, 37. *His own soul.* τὴν ψυχὴν αὐτοῦ· 'His own life.' So also in Matt. xvi. 26. The same word is rendered *life* in the preceding verse; and it is a violent and unnatural perversion of the common uses of language to suppose the same word to be employed so differently in the same argument. The sentiment of the passage may be illustrated by Job ii. 4.

Ib. 38. *Whosoever therefore.* ὃς γὰρ ἄν. 'For who-soever.' There is no conceivable reason for deviating from the letter of the original. See Matth. xvi. 27, Luke ix. 26.

x. 14. (= Matt. xix. 14.) *For of such is the kingdom of God.* τῶν γὰρ τοιούτων ἐστὶν ἡ βασιλεία τοῦ Θεοῦ. 'For to such belongeth the kingdom of God.' The common trans-lation is at best ambiguous; but probably no one, who should first become acquainted with the sentiment from the Greek, would hesitate to affix to the words the sense expressed by the proposed rendering. The construction is the same as in Matthew v. 3, *Theirs is the kingdom of heaven.*—A correct translation here is not unimportant to the question at issue between Baptists and their opponents.

Ib. 40. See on Matth. xx. 23.

xii. 32. *Thou hast said the truth; for there is*—ἐπ' ἀληθείας εἶπας, ὅτι—ἐστι—'Thou hast said truly, that there is'—

xiii. 9. *For they shall deliver you up to councils; and in the synagogues ye shall be beaten.* παραδώσουσι γὰρ ὑμᾶς εἰς συνέδρια καὶ εἰς συναγωγὰς δαρήσεσθε. 'For they shall deliver you up to councils and to synagogues; *and* ye shall be beaten.' It is most unlikely that εἰς συνέδρια and εἰς συναγωγὰς should be thus connected together both by juxta-position and the use of the same preposition, only to be disjoined and brought into different forms of expression, as in our translation. The parallel place in Luke, xxi. 12, is παραδιδόντες εἰς συναγωγὰς καὶ φυλακάς. Dr Doddridge's paraphrase of εἰς συναγωγὰς is, "the inferior courts in the synagogues." Compare Acts xxvi. 11. The want of the copula before δαρήσεσθε seems to have misled our Translators, as well as many editors, and Griesbach among them; but though I have inserted it in the proposed version, any one upon consulting the original will perhaps consider the omission of it *there* not only allowable, but emphatic.

Ib. 28. *Putteth forth leaves.* ἐκφύῃ τὰ φύλλα. 'Putteth forth its leaves.' Bishop Middleton would correct the translation by making τὰ φύλλα the nominative case

(*the leaves shoot forth*). The Reader may choose between
the two, comparing the parallel passage in Luke xxi. 30.
—At the beginning of the present verse the Article before
παραβολὴν has a similar emphasis: *Learn from the fig-tree*
its *parable;* i. e. *the parable* which it holds out.

Ib. 29. *Come to pass.* γινόμενα. 'Coming to pass.'
Compare the same expression in Luke xxi. 31. with v. 28
of the same chapter: ἀρχομένων τούτων γίνεσθαι.

xiv. 3. *Of spikenard.* νάρδου πιστικῆς. The margin
supplies two variations; *pure nard,* and *liquid nard.* The
former of these is espoused by Parkhurst, the latter by
Schleusner. The analogy of classical usage is undoubtedly more in favour of the latter than the former sense.
It remains however to be considered with regard to the
common translation, *spikenard,* that St Mark's frequent
practice of using Latin words may go far towards justify-
ing the supposition, which many critics have adopted, of
πιστικὸς being formed by a metathesis from *spicata.*—
The same combination of words occurs in John xii. 3.

Ib. 49. *But the scriptures must be fulfilled.* ἀλλ' ἵνα
πληρωθῶσιν αἱ γραφαί. 'But *this is done* that the scriptures may be fulfilled.' Our Translators seem to have
understood δεῖ or some similar word before ἵνα, which can
hardly be reconciled with analogy, unless they had completed it with ταῦτα γενέσθαι, *these things must be done,*
that—See on Matth. xxvi. 56.

Ib. 69. *A maid.* ἡ παιδίσκη. 'The maid.' There is
undoubtedly some difficulty in reconciling the little dis-
crepancies in the various accounts of this incident; and

if this difficulty were entirely removed by sacrificing here the principles of the Greek Article, one might be at least strongly tempted to do it. But it is hardly at all diminished by it. The occasion of the *second* denial is assigned by Matthew to "another maid," by Mark to the same "maid," by Luke to "another man," and by John to the general body of by-standers; which last circumstance, as including all the rest, may be considered as reconciling them all. To this effect there is a good note of Michaelis quoted by Middleton *in loco*.

xv. 6. *He released.* ἀπέλυεν. 'He used to release.' Matthew says more explicitly, εἰώθει ἀπολύειν, but Mark expresses the same thing more briefly by the imperfect tense.

Ib. 29. *Railed on him.* ἐβλασφήμουν αὐτόν. 'Reviled him'—if only for the sake of retaining the same trans· lation which is given to the same word in Matt. xxvii. 39.

Ib. 43. *Which also waited.* ὃς καὶ αὐτὸς ἦν προσδεχό- μενος. 'Who himself also was waiting.' This literal translation may seem to make a difficulty; for where is the opposition intended to be marked by the emphasis, *himself also ?* Evidently, between his secret discipleship (compare John xix. 38) and the more open avowal of pious women mentioned in v. 40-1. And the correct translation here proposed is adopted by our Translators in Luke xxiii. 51, notwithstanding the appearance of difficulty.

xvi. 14. *Unto the eleven as they sat at meat* (Marg. *sat together*). ἀνακειμένοις αὐτοῖς τοῖς ἕνδεκα. 'Unto the eleven themselves as they sat at meat.' Did our Translators intend by the marginal reading *together* to express some how or another the meaning of αὐτοῖς? However this be, it is plain that αὐτοῖς was the stumbling-block. I conceive it to refer to the difference between this and his former appearances. In them he had appeared only to individuals, and had sent messages by them to the eleven: (compare Matt. xxviii. 10, and other passages:) now he appeared to "the eleven themselves."

ST. LUKE.

CHAP. i. 9. *When he went.* εἰσελθών. 'Going.'

Ib. 20. *Thou believest.* ἐπίστευσας. 'Thou believedst.' So, I believe, all the versions except the authorised.

Ib. 48. *Shall call me blessed.* μακαριοῦσί με. 'Shall call me happy.' Let us hear the unseasonable vaunt of the Roman Catholic church upon this pious declaration of the Virgin: "These words are a prediction of that honour which the church in all ages should pay to the blessed Virgin. Let Protestants examine whether they are any way concerned in this prophecy." Note in the Douay Bible.—Now, will it be believed, that this simple word, upon which these learned annotators ground the claim of the Virgin to divine honours, occurs in James v. 11, in a sense too plain to be mistaken? *Behold, we count them happy* (or, *call them blessed*) *which endure.* ἰδοὺ μακαρίζομεν τοὺς ὑπομένοντας. In both places it predicates not honour, but happiness.—There is not a shadow of objection to the received translation in the passage of Luke, but that which arises from its awful abuse by the Papists.

ii. 7. *In a manger.* ἐν τῇ φάτνῃ. 'In the manger.' The force of the Article is obvious enough; but whether φάτνη should be otherwise translated, is a question ably discussed in a note of Bishop Middleton.

Ib. 22. *They brought him.* ἀνήγαγον αὐτόν. 'They brought him up'—as in v. 42, *they went up.*

Ib. 34. *For the fall and rising again of many.* εἰς πτῶσιν καὶ ἀνάστασιν πολλῶν. 'For the fall and rising of many.' The *rising again* would imply rising after their fall, and so refer it to the same persons; whereas the original means, I suppose, the falling of some and rising of others.

Ib. 38. *Coming in.* ἐπιστᾶσα. 'Standing near.' The common translation apparently contradicts the statement of the preceding verse, that she *departed not from the temple.*

iii. 14. *The soldiers.* στρατευόμενοι. '*Some* soldiers,' or '*some* on military service.' It is strange that our Translators should here have inserted the Article, when they had properly omitted it before τελῶναι, v. 12, and when, if it had been in the original, there would certainly have been a difficulty in explaining it.

Ib. 16. *One mightier.* ὁ ἰσχυρότερος. 'He that is mightier.'

iv. 26, 27. *Save, saving.* εἰ μή. 'But.' The mistake in the authorised translation is not an unnatural one, but

2

the effect of it is most unfortunate. It introduces a direct blunder by making the passage state, that Elias was sent to none of the Israelitish widows *except* to a Sidonian widow. And so of the lepers.—But the fact is, that though the natural and common sense of ἐι μὴ is *except*, it is also not uncommonly used, as here proposed, in a sense not of limitation, but exclusion. So, Galat. ii. 16. *A man is not justified by the works of the law, but* (ἐὰν μὴ) *by the faith of Jesus Christ;* where the learned Bishop of Salisbury has mistaken the sense of the particles*. A remarkable example of this exclusive use of ἐι μὴ occurs in Rev. xxi. 27, ἐι μὴ οἱ γεγραμμένοι ἐν τῷ βιβλίῳ τῆς ζωῆς τοῦ ἀρνίου. So in Aristophanes, Equit. 185, 6.

μῶν ἐκ καλῶν εἶ κἀγαθῶν;—μὰ τοὺς θεοὺς,

εἰ μὴ 'κ πονηρῶν γ'—

as the reading is admirably restored by Professor Bekker. —I will not enter further into this criticism here, having more fully investigated it in my remarks on Bishop Burgess's translation of the passage in Galatians†; but will only stop to remark, that this use of ἐι μὴ appears to be elliptical. *Are you born of good parents?—No,* (I am not born of any) *except base ones.*

Ib. 36. *What a word is this! for*—τίς ὁ λόγος οὗτος, ὅτι—'What *is* this word, that'—

v. 6. *Brake.* διερρήγνυτο. 'Began to break'—as in the next verse βυθίζεσθαι, *began to sink.*

---

* The late Bishop Burgess, Primary Charge, 1828, p. 79.
† Preface to Two Sermons on Justification by Faith, pp. 30, 35—7.

Ib. 30. *Their scribes and Pharisees.* οἱ γραμματεῖς αὐτῶν καὶ οἱ Φαρισαῖοι. 'The scribes and Pharisees of them,' or, 'among them.' Not, as the common version expresses it, The scribes and Pharisees belonging to them; but, those among them who were scribes and Pharisees. So Matthew xiv. 14, ἐθεράπευσε τοὺς ἀρρώστους αὐτῶν, where again it is translated *their sick.* Precisely similar is the use of αὐτῶν in Thucyd. IV. 126, προηγώνισθε τοῖς Μακεδόσιν αὐτῶν—*with the Macedonians of them,* i. e. with some of them, viz. the Macedonians.

Ib. 36. *The piece that was* taken *out of the new.* ἐπί- βλημα τὸ ἀπὸ τοῦ καινοῦ. 'The piece that was put in from the new'—or even, 'the piece of the new that was put in.'

vi. 1. *On the second sabbath after the first.* ἐν σαβ- βάτῳ δευτεροπρώτῳ. ' On the first sabbath after the second day of unleavened bread.' Our own translation of this very difficult expression is so unsatisfactory, neither, as Campbell observes, following the letter of the original, nor giving us words that convey any determinate sense, that in any proposed revision of the text some alteration must be attempted. I have adopted the rendering of Doddridge, whose note may be consulted; but am unable to add any thing to confirm the hypothesis. The opinions of learned men are much divided on the subject; but, perhaps, the weight of authority is on this side.

Ib. 34. *To receive.* ἀπολαβεῖν. 'To receive in return.' So in the next verse, μηδὲν ἀπελπίζοντες is, I think, rightly rendered, *hoping for nothing again;* though Campbell would correct it, *nothing despairing.*

Ib. 38. *Shall men give.* δώσουσιν. 'Shall *men* give.'
There could be no possible objection to the literal rendering here, *shall they give;* but as it is an idiom of frequent
occurrence, there are several instances in which the literal
rendering would be inadmissible. See Matth. v. 11, vii.
16, ix. 17, &c. The force of such expressions is clear from
this passage, in which δώσουσιν stands between δοθήσεται
and ἀντιμετρηθήσεται. It is equivalent to, *good measure shall
be given.*

vii. 3, 5. *The elders, a synagogue.* πρεσβυτέρους, τὴν
συναγωγήν. 'Elders, or *some* elders; our synagogue.' Indeed, a further correction should be applied to the latter
verse: 'and himself built us our synagogue.' The αὐτὸς
was probably intended to express, that he built it at his
own expense; but certainly on every account the *hath*
should be expunged before *built.*——In these two instances,
then, we have first the Article needlessly inserted; and
then omitted, not only needlessly, but clearly to the prejudice of the sense. And so common and easy is it κακὸν
κακῷ ἰᾶσθαι,—when the Article had been thrust out, it
became necessary to thrust in the sign of the perfect tense
before the aorist.

Ib. 38. *With tears.* τοῖς δάκρυσι. 'With her tears.'
The force of the Article in the sense referred to on
Matth. ix. 10, will be obvious to every reader.

ix. 24. *For whosoever will save…but whosoever will lose.*
ὃς γὰρ ἂν θέλῃ…σῶσαι…ὃς δ' ἂν ἀπολέσῃ. 'For whosoever
shall desire to save…but whosoever shall lose.' The difference in the original, which is very striking, is not mark-

ed in our translation. The selfish but fruitless desire to save life shall expose the man to condemnation; but the actual suffering of martyrdom shall be rewarded with life eternal.

Ib. 32. *And when they were awake.* διαγρηγορήσαντες δέ. 'And when they awoke.'

Ib. 55. *Ye know not what manner of spirit ye are of.* οὐκ οἴδατε οἵου πνεύματός ἐστε ὑμεῖς. 'Ye know not to what spirit ye belong:' i. e. what spirit is required of YOU, in accordance with the new dispensation now introduced by me, so different from that under which Elijah called down the fire from heaven. Compare ver. 56. That the common translation, as popularly understood, is wrong, I think there can be no doubt: it quite obliterates the emphasis, marked in the position of ὑμεῖς. Nor have I any hesitation as to the correction here proposed, though the terms in which it is expressed are not very satisfactory. In favour of the general view here taken, see Whitby's comment on the passage.

xi. 14. *The dumb spake.* ἐλάλησεν ὁ κωφός. 'The dumb *man* spake.' This is necessary to distinguish it as the action of *the man* released from the power of the *dumb devil* mentioned before: αὐτὸ ἦν κωφόν. On a subject sufficiently mysterious in itself it is important to avoid all ambiguity in the language. A very striking illustration of this division of action between the evil spirit and the man possessed by him occurs in Mark ix. 20. καὶ ἤνεγκαν αὐτὸν (the possessed man) πρὸς αὐτόν (to Jesus)· καὶ ἰδὼν αὐτὸν (the possessed man seeing Jesus), εὐθέως τὸ πνεῦμα ἐσπάραξεν αὐτὸν, καὶ (the possessed man) πεσὼν ἐπὶ τῆς γῆς ἐκυλίετο ἀφρίζων. The irregular construction of the middle clause makes no difficulty, being varied for an obvious reason from ἐσπαράχθη ὑπὸ τοῦ πνεύματος.

xii. 1. *First of all.* πρῶτον. 'First.' From the position of πρῶτον in the original there is a slight ambiguity, which has led some persons to connect it (improperly) with προσέχετε following. The common translation seems to favour an error of a different kind, as if our Lord had given his disciples this caution *first of all*, in reference to other instructions to follow afterwards. The real force of πρῶτον will appear from observing, that our Lord's teaching in this chapter divides itself into two parts; the one addressed to his own disciples, the other to the mixed multitude: he spoke to his disciples first, v. 1, then to the multitude, v. 15, in consequence of the question in v. 13. —Again in v. 22, he turns to his disciples, and in v. 54, again to the people. The difference in the character of the teaching addressed to the two classes of hearers is very observable.—Perhaps in this first verse the word *first* might be advantageously transposed: 'he began to say first to his disciples.'

Ib. 58. *When thou goest.* ὡς γὰρ ὑπάγεις. 'For as thou art going.' Another instance of the omission of the conjunction, though its use here is obvious, as illustrating the necessity for *discerning the time.* Compare Matth. v. 25.

xvi. 8. *And the lord commended.* καὶ ἐπῄνεσεν ὁ κύριος. 'And the master commended.' It would be better to preserve the same throughout the parable : the word *lord* is ambiguous, and is apt to confound the master of the steward with the divine speaker.

Ib. 12. *Another man's.* ἀλλοτρίῳ. 'Another's.' The word *man* is in several instances improperly supplied, where the original is more general. It may be questioned whether the reference here be not more directly to God, as the great proprietor who entrusts riches as a talent, and only indirectly to our fellow-men as those for whose benefit the talent is to be employed.

Ib. 19. *There was a certain rich man.* ἄνθρωπος δέ τις ἦν πλούσιος. 'But there was a certain rich man.' The different parts of this chapter appear to a cursory reader to be unconnected with each other; and our translators by omitting the δέ in this verse have certainly not assisted us towards discerning the connexion.—In the first application of the parable of the unjust steward, our Lord had given some general lessons on the right use of worldly riches, to v. 12; and in v. 13 he enforced the principle by insisting on an undivided devotion to the service of God, the great Master, and especially condemned the service of Mammon (worldly gain) as incompatible with it. This offended "the Pharisees, who were covetous;" and, being interrupted by their derision, Christ suspended the regular course of his instruction to reply to them, from v. 15 to 18. The scope of this passage seems to be the following: You *justify yourselves before men,* and make a great shew of righteousness by your zeal for the law, which you falsely charge me with undervaluing. This, however, I am so far from doing, that I declare that *heaven and earth* might

more *easily pass away than one tittle of the law fail:* but the
dispensation of the law was only to last till the time of
John; and since then *the kingdom of God is preached.*
But now, to shew further that I am no enemy to the holiness of the law, and that your professed zeal for it is only
a hypocritical pretence, I declare that you pervert it, and
relax the obligations of its holiness by your traditionary
glosses on the subject of marriage and divorce (compare
Matth. xix. 3, and Deuteron. xxiv. 1); and I maintain,
that to put away a wife on such pretexts as you allow of,
is so contrary to the purity of God's law, that it is nothing
better than adultery.——Having thus rebuked them, he
returns to his main purpose, viz. the application of the
parable to the subject of riches: *But* (v. 19), leaving the
cavils of these covetous and self-righteous objectors, I will
illustrate what I mean by faithfulness in the unrighteous
mammon (v. 11) by the affecting case of one who was
unfaithful. *There was a certain rich man.*——

xvii. 17. *Were there not ten cleansed?* οὐχὶ οἱ δέκα
ἐκαθαρίσθησαν; 'Were not the ten cleansed?'

xviii. 11. *The Pharisee stood and prayed thus with
himself.* ὁ Φαρισαῖος σταθεὶς πρὸς ἑαυτὸν ταῦτα προσηύχετο.
'The Pharisee standing by himself prayed thus.' The
order of the words and the sense are both in favour of
the change. To say merely that he *stood,* is tame: *standing
by himself* exactly illustrates the Pharisee's character, as
drawn in Isai. lxv. 5. Again, it is more in character to
utter such a prayer aloud than *with himself.*

Ib. 42. *Hath saved thee.* σέσωκέ σε. 'Hath made thee
whole.' So translated chap. xvii. 19, and without entering

on the question, whether any spiritual benefit accompanied the bodily healing or not, it is desirable to retain the uniformity of the original. Compare Acts iv. 9.

xix. 3. *Who he was.* τίς ἐστι. 'What sort of a person he was.' The same sense as ὁποῖος ἦν, James i. 24.

Ib. 11. *He added and spake.* προσθεὶς · εἶπε. 'He farther spake.' The Hebraism is very awkward in the English, though adopted in the Greek.

Ib. 31. *Because the Lord hath need of him.* Ὅτι ὁ Κύριος αὐτοῦ χρείαν ἔχει. 'The Lord—or, The Master— hath need of him.' The very same words are so rendered in Matth. xxi. 3, and in Mark xi. 3 a little differently; thus presenting three varieties in the three Evangelists. The pleonastic ὅτι here is merely the common mode of introducing a speech in the New Testament. See ver. 42, ὅτι εἰ ἔγνως, and numberless other instances. It would seem to be more proper in these cases to put the capital letter not to the ὅτι, but to the following word, which is in fact the beginning of the speech. The mode of expression is a blending of two modes, the direct and oblique —*he said, I will go,* and, *he said that he would go:* the ὅτι belongs to the oblique form, which then passes into the direct.—In ver. 34, where the disciples do what is here commanded, the direct form occurs simply, Ὁ Κύριος without ὅτι. The English language does not admit of blending the two modes.

xx. 36. *Neither.* οὔτε γάρ. 'For neither.' The great use of the conjunction here needs no explanation.

xxi. 9. *By and by.* εὐθέως. 'Immediately.' Matth. xiii. 21.

xxii. 29. *And I appoint unto you a kingdom, as my Father hath appointed unto me, that ye may eat and drink.* κἀγὼ διατίθεμαι ὑμῖν, καθὼς διέθετό μοι ὁ πατήρ μου βασιλείαν, ἵνα ἐσθίητε καὶ πίνητε. 'And I appoint unto you, as my Father hath appointed me a kingdom, to eat and drink.' That is, I appoint you *to eat and drink in my kingdom.* The kingdom being given to Christ, he assigns to his servants their portion in it.—Griesbach indeed places a comma before βασιλείαν, but, I. think, to the manifest injury of the sense; and this arrangement fixes a stronger emphasis on the enclitic μοι than it will naturally bear. Whether the sentiment expressed in our version be scriptural, is not the question; but whether this passage is intended to express it.

Ib. 36. *And he that hath no sword, let him sell his garment, and buy one.* καὶ ὁ μὴ ἔχων πωλησάτω τὸ ἱμάτιον αὐτοῦ, καὶ ἀγορασάτω μάχαιραν. 'And he that hath none, let him sell his garment, and buy a sword.' In the prospect of the coming dangers, let him *that hath a purse, take it,* viz. to buy a sword with; *and he that hath no* purse, *let him sell his* very *garment* for the same purpose. The ὁ μὴ ἔχων is so manifestly opposed to the preceding ὁ ἔχων, that it seems strangely perplexing not to understand the same object after it. Wicliffe followed the right construction: Tyndale misled Cranmer and King James's translators.

Ib. 69. *Hereafter.* ἀπὸ τοῦ νῦν. 'Henceforth.' The same remark applies to ἀπ' ἄρτι, Matth. xxvi. 64, and John i. 51. Not that there is any real difference between the two words, *hereafter* signifying *after this time,* and *henceforth, from this time :* but in common usage *hereafter* is generally understood of a period more remote. See the note on John xiii. 7.

xxiii. 15. *Is done unto him.* ἐστι πεπραγμένον αὐτῷ. 'Is done by him'—i. e. by Christ: in the other case it must be, unto Herod. Compare Acts xxv. 11.

Ib. 32. *Two others, malefactors.* ἕτεροι δύο κακοῦργοι. 'Two other malefactors.' What is here proposed, is indeed the reading of our Translators, as found in the early editions ; but some modern copies read it as quoted above, and others again, clumsily enough, *Two other, male-factors*—to avoid what appears the natural conclusion from the more simple form of expression. The import of the original, however, is clear enough from comparing as an example Plato Euthyd. § 5. ὅ τ' Εὐθύδημος καὶ ὁ Διονυσόδωρος καὶ ἄλλοι μαθηταὶ ἅμα πολλοί—where the sense evidently is, 'many disciples *besides*'—i. e. disciples of Euthydemus and Dionysodorus.

Ib. 40. *Dost not thou fear God?* οὐδὲ φοβῇ σὺ τὸν Θεόν; 'Dost not even thou fear God?' *Ne tu quidem*—even thou in thy circumstances of desperate wretchedness, whatever others may do in the unthinking levity of present security?

Ib. 42. *Into thy kingdom.* ἐν τῇ βασιλείᾳ σου. 'In thy kingdom.'

Ib. 44. *All the earth.* ὅλην τὴν γῆν. 'All the land'—as in the margin, and in Matth. xxvii. 45.

Ib. 46. *And when Jesus had cried with a loud voice, he said.* καὶ φωνήσας φωνῇ μεγάλῃ ὁ Ἰησοῦς εἶπε. 'And

Jesus cried with a loud voice, and said.' When, as in the present case, a participle and verb are combined together both in the past tense, the action described by the participle may be either antecedent to that of the verb, or coincident with it; and the sense alone must determine the point. In this passage it is not intended, I conceive, to be stated, that Jesus first cried out something else, and then uttered the words here recorded, which is what our translation expresses; but that he uttered these words with a loud voice.

xxiv. 10. *And other* women that were *with them.* καὶ αἱ λοιπαὶ σὺν αὐταῖς. 'And the other *women* with them.' The common translation leaves the matter sufficiently indefinite, when it was the express object of the Evangelist here to state who they were that carried these tidings to the Apostles. And the original is definite. But who, it will be asked, were THE *others?* I answer, that company of women who along with the two Maries and Joanna are mentioned so frequently and so honourably in this history. Luke viii. 2—3. xxiii. 49, 55. xxiv. 22.

Ib. 12. *Departed wondering in himself.* ἀπῆλθε πρὸς ἑαυτὸν θαυμάζων. 'Departed to his home wondering.' So John xx. 10, ἀπῆλθον οὖν πάλιν πρὸς ἑαυτοὺς οἱ μαθηταὶ, where the same circumstance is related of the *two* disciples, Peter and John, and where, happily, the original has no ambiguity. Compare also Matth. xxvi. 57, πρὸς Καϊά-φαν τὸν ἀρχιερέα, ὅπου, with Luke xxii. 54.

Ib. 44. *Which were written.* τὰ γεγραμμένα. 'Which are written.'

ST. JOHN.

CHAP. I. 9. *Which lighteth every man that cometh into the world.* ὃ φωτίζει πάντα ἄνθρωπον ἐρχόμενον εἰς τὸν κόσμον. 'Which coming into the world enlighteneth every man.' The sense expressed by the authorised translation would properly require τὸν before ἐρχόμενον. This objection might be met by translating ἐρχόμενον *at his coming.* Still it is more natural to refer ἐρχόμενον εἰς τὸν κόσμον to the φῶς, than to πάντα ἄνθρωπον· for in the latter case it hardly expresses any thing, whereas in the former it reminds us of the distinctive character of the Messiah, so frequently mentioned by St John, ὁ ἐρχόμενος. The second rendering I have mentioned conveys a very questionable sense.—If it be still asked, What is the meaning of the declaration contained in the passage? I answer, that it appears to me to repeat, only a little more emphatically, the statement of the fourth verse, *The life was the light of men.* The new translation, too, makes it more general than the old.

It may be observed, that in v. 8, our Translators have not improved the original by twice changing *the light* into *that light.* See on Matth. xv. 12.

Ib. 12. *The sons of God.* τέκνα Θεοῦ. 'Sons of God.'

Ib. 51. *Hereafter.* ἀπ' ἄρτι. 'Henceforth.' This is clearly the proper sense of the words, and I believe they are no where in the New Testament translated other-

wise*. (John xiii. 19 is an exception; but see the margin.)
I understand, therefore, our Saviour's words to mean,
that the Gospel-dispensation was now commenced, and
that henceforward, from this time, they should behold
fulfilled in him the blessings which had been represented
in Jacob's vision (Gen. xxviii. 12), and which they had
been looking for as belonging to that dispensation.

iii. 10. *Art thou a master of Israel*—σὺ εἶ ὁ διδάσκαλος
τοῦ ᾿Ισραήλ—'Art thou the *famous* master of Israel'—
That such is really the import of the words, can hardly
be doubted. It is excellently illustrated by Bishop Middleton; and in a similar way, by a reference to the high-
sounding titles which the Jews used to give their Rabbies,
we must interpret chap. v. 35, THE *burning and shining
light.*

Ib. 25. *Between some of John's disciples and the Jews.*
ἐκ τῶν μαθητῶν ᾿Ιωάννου μετὰ ᾿Ιουδαίων. 'Between John's
disciples and the Jews;' or more literally, 'on the part of
John's disciples with the Jews.' Such I conceive to be the
force of the preposition ἐκ here: that assigned it by our
Translators is hardly admissible after ἐγένετο ζήτησις.

iv. 29. *Is not this the Christ?* μήτι οὗτός ἐστιν ὁ Χριστός;
'Is this the Christ?' So, v. 33, μήτις, *hath any man*—not,
hath not—The same correction is required in chap. xviii.
17, 25. In Matthew xii. 23, I would translate also, *Is*

---

* I had overlooked Matth. xxvi. 64, where ἀπ' ἄρτι is rendered
hereafter, as is ἀπὸ τοῦ νῦν also in the corresponding passage,
Luke xxii. 69. St. Luke's expression shews conclusively the proper
meaning of the phrase. See the note there.

this—instead of, *Is not this*—(Such, indeed, is the reading of the earlier editions of our version.) Both the translations express the same thing in the result; but the omission of the negative gives a livelier force to the mode of conveying it. The μὴ thus joined to an indicative implies here a mixture of belief, doubt, and wonder. Compare vii. 41. Acts x. 47. Οὐχ οὗτός ἐστι, vii. 25, is properly rendered, *Is not this*—So 1 Cor. ix. 4, μὴ οὐκ ἔχομεν, *Have we not?*

Ib. 37. *Herein is that saying true.* ἐν τούτῳ ὁ λόγος ἐστὶν ὁ ἀληθινός. 'Herein is *exemplified* the true saying,' as Middleton.—Many passages, in which a slight correction is required on account of the Article, I pass over in order to avoid sameness, and the repetition of what that learned Prelate has done already.

v. 22. *For the Father judgeth no man.* οὐδὲ γὰρ ὁ πατὴρ κρίνει οὐδένα. 'For neither doth the Father judge any man.' The word οὐδὲ marks the introduction of another proof or illustration of the equality of the Son with the Father.

Ib. 39. *Search the scriptures; for*—ἐρευνᾶτε τὰς γραφὰς ὅτι—'Ye search the scriptures, because'—This reading appears to me to give a clearer sense to the passage itself, and to mark more distinctly its connexion with what has gone before. Had the assigned reason been, 'for in them ye *have* eternal life,' or 'in them ye *may find* eternal life,' it would have furnished an obvious ground for the exhortation to *search* them; but if they *thought* and acknowledged that they had eternal life in them, this exhortation may seem to be superfluous. In the other case the tenor of the words is plain : You are in the habit of searching the scriptures; and why? because you believe that you have eternal life in them: and these scriptures which you so carefully search *are they which testify of me* as the Saviour that is to give you that life; and yet you are not willing to come to me that you may obtain it.

The connexion is this : Christ had said in v. 31, *If I bear witness of myself, my witness is not true.* He proceeds to obviate this objection by appealing to the testimony of his Father, vv. 32, 37; John the Baptist, 33; his own miracles, 36; and all these appeals are in the declaratory form : *Ye sent unto John,* &c. so, *Ye search the scriptures—* as it is clear they did do, for their contradictions against Christ were derived from a perverse or ignorant interpretation of them.

The Roman Catholics of course prefer the rendering I have recommended; but it cannot help them much in the way of discountenancing the general reading of the scriptures, as in the place of a direct command to that effect, which was not necessary, it substitutes a practical example, quoted by our Lord with implied approbation, though accompanied with a censure of their perverse misunderstanding of what they read.

vi. 33. *He which cometh down.* ὁ καταβαίνων. 'That which cometh down'—viz. the bread, ἄρτος. The great truth of himself being this bread, or of its being any personal substance, is not opened by our Lord till the 35th verse, in answer to the petition of v. 34. Compare ver.

41, where the Jews murmur at our Lord's saying, *I am the bread*, &c.; whereas the declaration of v. 33 provoked no murmuring, but led them to pray for the bread that came down from heaven.

Ib. 40. *May have everlasting life; and I will raise him up at the last day.* ἔχῃ ζωὴν αἰώνιον, καὶ ἀναστήσω αὐτὸν ἐγὼ τῇ ἐσχάτῃ ἡμέρᾳ. 'Should have everlasting life, and *that* I should raise him up at the last day.' That ἀναστήσω is not a future indicative, but an aorist conjunctive, is clear from an inspection of ver. 39; and so the connexion is, ἵνα πᾶς ἔχῃ, καὶ ἐγὼ ἀναστήσω.

Ib. 48. *That bread.* ὁ ἄρτος. 'The bread.' So, vv. 58, 69, 'the bread,' 'the Christ.'

Ib. 51. *And the bread that I will give is my flesh.* καὶ ὁ ἄρτος δὲ ὃν ἐγὼ δώσω ἡ σάρξ μου ἐστίν. 'And moreover the bread which I will give is my flesh.' The omission of the particle δὲ in our translation seems to me to obliterate one of the way-marks which our Lord has given to guide us through the intricacies of this discussion. The points of it are opened in regular succession; and the insertion of δὲ in this verse marks clearly the transition from one to another of them: (1) I will *give* the meat or bread of life, v. 27. (2) *I am myself* the bread of life, v. 35. (3) How? by giving my flesh for the life of the world, v. 51, i. e. by dying for it.

Ib. 62. *What and if.* ἐὰν οὖν. '*What* then if.'

vii. 17. *Will do.* θέλῃ ποιεῖν. 'Desire to do,' or, 'be willing.'

Ib. 22. *Not because.* οὐχ ὅτι. 'Not that.'

3

Ib. 41. *Shall Christ*—μὴ γὰρ Χριστός—'What, doth Christ'—See on Matt. xxvii. 23.

viii. 1. *Jesus went.* Ἰησοῦς δὲ ἐπορεύθη. 'But Jesus went.' The insertion of the copula shews that this verse should be connected with the preceding chapter.

Ib. 44. *When he speaketh a lie, he speaketh of his own; for he is a liar, and the father of it.* ὅταν λαλῇ τὸ ψεῦδος, ἐκ τῶν ἰδίων λαλεῖ· ὅτι ψεύστης ἐστὶ καὶ ὁ πατὴρ αὐτοῦ. 'When *a man* speaketh falsehood, he speaketh of his own; for his father also is a liar.' The chief part of this correction is Bishop Middleton's; and no less necessary, and still more obvious, is the remaining part. The Bishop translated, *for he is a liar, and* so *is his father:* but after describing the man as *speaking a lie,* it was superfluous to add, *for he is a liar.*—The only questionable point in the criticism is the supplying a nominative before λαλῇ. But the omission of τις in such a case is warranted by the example of the best authors; and our own Translators have considered it to be so omitted, perhaps unnecessarily, in Hebrews x. 38. The meaning of ἐκ τῶν ἰδίων, *of his own,* is sufficiently clear. Bishop Middleton's paraphrase is, *after the manner of his kindred.*

Ib. 56. *Rejoiced to see.* ἠγαλλιάσατο ἵνα ἴδῃ. 'Earnestly desired to see.' The other translation is hardly free from the charge of tautology.

ix. 40. *Some of the Pharisees which were with him.* ἐκ τῶν Φαρισαίων οἱ ὄντες μετ' αὐτοῦ. 'Those of the Pharisees who were with him.'

x. 11.   *Giveth his life.*   τὴν ψυχὴν αὐτοῦ . τίθησιν.
'Layeth down his life'—because so translated in v.
15. .

Ib. 15.   *As the Father knoweth me, even so I know the
Father.*   καθὼς γινώσκει με ὁ Πατὴρ, κἀγὼ γινώσκω τὸν
πατέρα.   'As the Father knoweth me, and I know the
Father.'   To the common translation, either as a translation, or as a doctrine, there can be no possible objection;
but the question is, how such a doctrine stated here falls
in with the scope of the passage, which is to set forth
the character of Christ as the good Shepherd.   In the
amended version (which, though not borrowed from
others, claims no credit on the ground of originality)
the connexion of the whole passage is clearly marked:
besides which the passage furnishes one of the most
striking and beautiful examples of *introverted parallelism* to be found in the whole volume of scripture.   Vv.
14, 15:

1. I am the good Shepherd:
   2. And I know my *sheep,*
      3. And am known of mine;
      3. As the Father knoweth me,
   2. And I know the Father:
1. And I lay down my life for the sheep.

Thus the whole passage is a mere expansion of what
had been said v. 11; and the first and last clauses, *I am
the good Shepherd*—and *I lay down my life for the sheep,*
are an exact repetition, word for word, of the two clauses
of that verse, the same term τίθημι being repeated in the

original, though unfortunately varied in our translation*.

Ib. 25. *And ye believed not.* καὶ οὐ πιστεύετε. (A
few copies however read ἐπιστεύετε or ἐπιστεύσατε.) 'And
ye believe not.' The Roman Catholic version follows this
reading, and so translates it: but it is joined with another
change in the preceding clause, which is any thing but an
improvement: 'I speak to you, and you believe not.'

Ib. 28. *Any man.* τις. 'Any.'

Ib. 29. *No man is able.* οὐδεὶς δύναται. 'None is
able.' See on Luke xvi. 12 †.

---

* Compare another example, Rev. iii. 21.

 ὁ νικῶν,
  δώσω αὐτῷ καθίσαι μετ' ἐμοῦ
  ἐν τῷ θρόνῳ μου,
  ὡς κἀγὼ ἐνίκησα
  καὶ ἐκάθισα μετὰ τοῦ Πατρός μου
  ἐν τῷ θρόνῳ αὐτοῦ.

Æsch. Eumen. 150—161, is not unworthy to be subjoined here, as
a singularly elegant example of antistrophic parallelism:

 ἐμοὶ δ' ὄνειδος ἐξ ὀνειράτων μολὸν   στρ.
  ἔτυψεν δίκαν διφρηλάτου
  μεσολαβεῖ κέντρῳ·
 ὑπὸ φρένας, ὑπὸ λοβὸν πάρεστι μαστίκτορος
  δαΐου δαμίου
  βαρὺ, τὸ περίβαρυ κρύος ἔχειν.
 τοιαῦτα δρῶσιν οἱ νεώτεροι θεοὶ,   ἀντ.
  κρατοῦντες τὸ πᾶν δίκας πλέον
  φονολιβῆ θρόνον·
 περὶ πόδα, περὶ κάρα πάρεστι γᾶς ὀμφαλὸν
  προσδρακεῖν αἱμάτων
  βλοσυρὸν ἀρόμενον ἄγος ἔχειν.

† In some editions the word *man* is printed in Italics, as if to
apprise the reader that it is not in the original; but it is not so dis-

xi. 6. *When he had heard therefore.* ὡς οὖν ἤκουσεν. 'When he heard then.' The οὖν appears to be inserted, as in many similar cases, merely for the purpose of resuming the narrative after its interruption by the parenthesis of the preceding verse; and can hardly warrant the use which good men have made of the English *therefore,* that *because* he loved him, *therefore* he delayed, &c. In fact, the repetition from v. 3, ἀκούσας, ὡς ἤκουσεν, seems to mark a direct continuation: Jesus received the message, made an observation upon it, and remained where he was.

Ib. 51, 52. *That nation.* τοῦ ἔθνους. 'The nation.'

xiii. 7. *But thou shalt know hereafter.* γνώσῃ δὲ μετὰ ταῦτα. 'But thou shalt know afterwards.' Literally, ' after these things;' i. e. when I have finished what I am doing; whereas *hereafter* would seem to imply a period more remote.

xviii. 15. *Another disciple.* ὁ ἄλλος μαθητής. 'The other disciple,' viz. John, the friend of Peter. See the highly interesting note of Bishop Middleton; and compare John xx. 2, 3, 4, 8, referred to by him. It should be observed also, that in chapter xx. 2, the words, *the other disciple whom Jesus loved,* are not to be taken in close con-

---

tinguished in the early editions, being considered by our Translators as included in the adjective. The translation here recommended is found in some versions prior to King James's, and has been introduced without authority in some subsequent ones, ex. gr. Field's, 1666. As early as 1647 (how much earlier, I am not aware) the Italics began to be introduced: a Bible printed by Barker in that year exhibits ' any *man*' in v. 28, but ' no man' in v. 29.

nexion, so as to imply that Peter and John were *the two*
disciples whom he loved; but there must be a kind of
break, as if the Evangelist had said, *the other disciple*—him
I mean *whom Jesus loved.*

Ib. 17. *Art not thou also*—μὴ καὶ σὺ εἶ—'Art thou
also'—See on chapter iv. 29. Apply the same remark to
v. 25.

THE ACTS OF THE APOSTLES.

CHAP. ii. 5. *And there were dwelling at Jerusalem Jews,
devout men.* ἦσαν δὲ ἐν Ἱερουσαλὴμ κατοικοῦντες Ἰουδαῖοι
ἄνδρες εὐλαβεῖς. 'And there were devout Jews dwelling
in Jerusalem.'

Ib. 40. *Save yourselves from this untoward generation.*
σώθητε ἀπὸ τῆς γενεᾶς τῆς σκολιᾶς ταύτης. 'Save yourselves
from among this untoward generation.' So in Rev. xiv.
4, *were redeemed from among men.* ἀπὸ τῶν ἀνθρώπων.
Compare also Galat. i. 4, and the note upon it. Perhaps
in the present passage the received translation is intended
to express the same thing; but it is not so clear.

iii. 19. *When.* ὅπως ἄν.—I am not prepared to recommend the change here contended for by some, *in order
that*, though undoubtedly it has great probability in its
favour. The authorised translation is at least an unusual
one; but before it be discarded on that ground, the following examples among others must be well considered:
Rom. xv. 24, ὡς ἐὰν πορεύωμαι εἰς τὴν Σπανίαν, ἐλεύσομαι

πρὸς ὑμᾶς. 1 Corinth. xi. 34, τὰ δὲ λοιπὰ, ὡς ἂν ἔλθω, δια-τάξομαι. Philipp. ii. 23, τοῦτον μὲν οὖν ἐλπίζω πέμψαι, ὡς ἂν ἀπίδω τὰ περὶ ἐμὲ, ἐξαυτῆς. Josh. ii. 14, Sept. ὡς ἂν παραδῷ Κύριος ὑμῖν τὴν πόλιν, ποιήσετε εἰς ἐμὲ ἔλεος καὶ ἀλή-θειαν*.—A correspondent reminds me, that the present passage is translated by Tertullian, de Resurr. Carn. c. XXIII. *Ut tempora vobis superveniant refrigerii.*

iv. 9. *By what means.* ἐν τίνι. 'By whom,' or 'through whom:' but this *form* must be preserved on account of ἐν τῷ ὀνόματι and ἐν τούτῳ answering to it in the next verse.

Ib. 21. *Finding nothing how they might punish them.* μηδὲν εὑρίσκοντες τὸ πῶς κολάσωνται αὐτούς. 'Finding no means of punishing them.' Dobree's correction is, *Finding no* witnesses.'

vii. 36. *After that he had shewed.* ποιήσας. 'Shew-ing.' See on Luke xxiii. 46. The common translation makes the *bringing out* subsequent to the miracles in the wilderness.

Ib. 45. *That came after.* διαδεξάμενοι. 'Having re-ceived by succession:' but perhaps the reading of the margin, *having received*, may be considered sufficient. The common translation must on every account be corrected.

Ib. 46. *A tabernacle for the God of Jacob.* σκήνωμα τῷ Θεῷ Ἰακώβ. 'A habitation for the God of Jacob'——

---

* They who doubt about the accuracy of rendering ὅπως *when,* like ὡς, should remember that the two words belong originally to the same family, and, with many other passages, should compare Hom. Odyss. III. 373, Soph. Antig. 253, 407, &c.

or, 'a place for the tabernacle of.'—It makes a strange confusion to say that Joshua brought the tabernacle into Canaan, and David afterwards desired to *find a tabernacle for God.* The words are quoted literally from the LXX. translation of Psal. cxxxii. 5. The former of the translations here proposed is that adopted in the Psalm; but the latter seems preferable as being more exact.

viii. 11. *Because that of long time he had .bewitched them with sorceries.* διὰ τὸ ἱκανῷ χρόνῳ ταῖς μαγείαις ἐξεστα⁺ κέναι αὐτούς. 'Because of a long time they had been bewitched with *his* sorceries.' The perfect ἐξεστακέναι does not admit a transitive sense.

Ib. 20. *Because thou hast thought that the gift of God may be purchased with money.* ὅτι τὴν δωρεὰν τοῦ Θεοῦ ἐνόμισας διὰ χρημάτων κτᾶσθαι. 'Because thou hast thought to purchase the gift of God with money.'

ix. 7. *A voice.* τῆς φωνῆς. 'The voice.'

Ib. 31. *And were edified; and walking in the fear of the Lord, and in the comfort of the Holy Ghost, were multiplied.* οἰκοδομούμεναι καὶ πορευόμεναι τῷ φόβῳ τοῦ Κυρίου, καὶ τῇ παρακλήσει τοῦ ἁγίου πνεύματος ἐπληθύνοντο. 'Being edified, and walking in the fear of the Lord; and were replenished with the comfort of the Holy Ghost.' The rendering here depends on the punctuation. I have adopted that of Griesbach, who however intimates by an asterisk, that it may be differently pointed; but such a difference of pointing would introduce a violent disruption between the two participles οἰκοδομούμεναι and πορευόμεναι, which, being unnecessary, it is certainly desirable to avoid.

x. 24. *Waited for them.* ἦν προσδοκῶν αὐτούς. 'Was waiting for them.' More literal and more clear.

Ib. 36—8. "*Male versa.*" DOBREE, Adversaria, vol. i. p. 569. I entirely agree in the opinion so briefly expressed by my learned predecessor; and greatly lament that he has not left behind him any intimation of the manner in which he would have translated the passage.—In the pre sent case, I will first lay before the Reader the original Greek, as I conceive it ought to be pointed, and then sub-join my own translation, followed by remarks.

Τὸν λόγον ὃν ἀπέστειλε τοῖς υἱοῖς Ἰσραὴλ, εὐαγγελιζόμενος εἰρήνην διὰ Ἰησοῦ Χριστοῦ, (οὗτός ἐστι πάντων κύριος,) ὑμεῖς οἴδατε·

τὸ γενόμενον ῥῆμα καθ᾽ ὅλης τῆς Ἰουδαίας, ἀρξάμενον ἀπὸ τῆς Γαλιλαίας, μετὰ τὸ βάπτισμα ὃ ἐκήρυξεν Ἰωάννης·

Ἰησοῦν τὸν ἀπὸ Ναζαρὲθ, ὡς ἔχρισεν αὐτὸν ὁ Θεὸς——

'The word which he sent to the children of Israel, preaching peace by Jesus Christ, (he is Lord of all,) ye know:

Even the matter which took place throughout all Judea, beginning from Galilee, after the baptism which John preached;

Concerning Jesus of Nazareth, how God anointed him'——

In the common version a strong objection lies against the two words λόγος and ῥῆμα being rendered by the same English term, *word*, and in such a way as if the latter were a mere repetition of the former. And the rendering of τὸ γενόμενον ῥῆμα by *the word which was published,* is perhaps still more objectionable. The translation also of ἀρξάμενον, *and began*, is a needless and awkward variation from the original.

In the proposed translation, it may perhaps seem to the English reader that the words *ye know* at the end of v. 36, especially as they are separated from the rest of the sentence by the parenthesis immediately preceding, are too feeble and languid to close such a sentence in such a manner. But by the Greek reader the words ὑμεῖς οἴδατε in that position will be acknowledged to possess a peculiar and appropriate emphasis. In fact, the insertion of the nominative ὑμεῖς seems to me to make the expression too emphatic to stand, as it did before, at the beginning of the following verse.—'Ρῆμα, properly signifying *a word*, signifies also, like the Hebrew דָּבָר, whether we call it a Hebraism or not, a *thing*, or *matter*, of which a *word* is the index: and so St. Luke uses it in his gospel, i. 37. Its connexion here with γενόμενον is alone almost sufficient to determine it to that sense. Compare Luke ii. 15, τὸ ῥῆμα τοῦτο τὸ γεγονός.—The other variations I have introduced, need no further explanation.

Ib. 39. *Whom they slew and hanged on a tree.* ὃν ἀνεῖλον κρεμάσαντες ἐπὶ ξύλου. 'Whom they hanged on a tree and slew:' or, 'whom they slew by hanging on a tree.' The singular inversion here introduced by our Translators can hardly have been any other than an oversight. Compare another example of the same singular mistake, chap. v. 30: ὃν ὑμεῖς διεχειρίσασθε κρεμάσαντες ἐπὶ ξύλου, *whom ye slew and hanged on a tree*. Of course,

when a verb with a copula is thus substituted for a participle, it ought to come in order before the other verb in
the sentence.

xi. 17.   *Unto us who believed.*   καὶ ἡμῖν πιστεύσασιν.
'Unto us also upon our believing.'   The common translation would properly require τοῖς before πιστεύσασιν.   But
it is not the object here to distinguish them from others
by the circumstance of their believing, but to refer to the
time when the Holy Ghost was given them as an evidence or fruit of their believing.   See Ephes. i. 13: *In
whom after that ye believed ye were sealed.*

Ib. 27.   *Came.* κατῆλθον.   'Came down.'

xii. 4.   *After Easter.* μετὰ τὸ πάσχα.   'After the
Passover.'

xiii. 27.   *Because they knew him not, nor yet the voices
of the prophets...they have fulfilled them in condemning
him.* τοῦτον ἀγνοήσαντες καὶ τὰς φωνὰς τῶν προφητῶν,...
κρίναντες ἐπλήρωσαν.   'Being ignorant of this *word* and
the voices of the prophets...fulfilled *it* by condemning
him.'   The words *they, have,* are both worse than superfluous.   *Fulfilled it,* this word: it might be *them,* the
voices of the prophets; but the other seems better on
account of the emphasis marked in τοῦτον, sc. τὸν λόγον
τῆς σωτηρίας, mentioned in the preceding verse.   If it had
been αὐτὸν instead of τοῦτον, it would have been ambiguous; either *him* (Jesus), or *it* (the word): but τοῦτον
can have no ambiguity.   And the *ignorance* expressed
in ἀγνοήσαντες must be interpreted, as in other places, of
not understanding.

xiv. 6. *They were ware of* it, *and fled.* συνιδόντες κατέφυγον. 'Having considered *it,* they fled.' If it had been an assault *meditated,* it might properly be said *they were ware of it;* but this is superfluous where it was *an assault made.* Συνιδὼν is rightly translated chap. xii. 12, as I have here corrected it. It means that they considered what was best to be done.

xv. 14. *How God at the first did visit.* καθὼς πρῶτον ὁ Θεὸς ἐπεσκέψατο. 'How God first visited.' It refers to the first occasion of God's visiting the Gentiles, not to his visiting them before the Jews.

Ib. 22. *To send chosen men of their own company.* 'κλεξαμένους ἄνδρας ἐξ αὐτῶν πέμψαι. 'To choose men out of their own company and send.' Literally, 'Having chosen men from among themselves to send.' So in v. 25.

xvi. 12. *Which is the chief city of that part of Macedonia,* and *a colony.* ἥτις ἐστὶ πρώτη τῆς μερίδος τῆς Μακεδονίας πόλις, κολωνία. 'Which is the chief of its district, a city of Macedonia, a colony.' This is the rendering proposed by Bishop Middleton, for want of a better; and I regret that I cannot furnish a better, though certainly not satisfied with this.

Ib. 22. *To beat* them. ῥαβδίζειν. 'To beat *them* with rods'—as it is translated 2 Cor. xi. 25, where this circumstance is referred to.

Ib. 27. *He drew out.* σπασάμενος. 'Drew.' The pronoun is redundant, and the preposition needless.

xvii. 9. *Of the other.* τῶν λοιπῶν. 'Of the rest.' The former rendering is ambiguous.

Ib. 15. *Receiving.* λαβόντες. 'Having received.' The other might seem to imply that they departed *in consequence of* receiving this commandment.

Ib. 23. *Ye ignorantly worship.* ἀγνοοῦντες εὐσεβεῖτε. ' Ye worship without knowing *him.*'

Ib. 29. *And hath made.* ἐποίησέ τε. 'And he hath made.' The common arrangement connects ἐποίησε improperly with the preceding participle διδούς. The construction is regular, οὐ κατοικεῖ οὐδὲ θεραπεύεται, ἐποίησέ τε.

xix. 2. *Whether there be any Holy Ghost.* εἰ πνεῦμα ἅγιον ἐστίν· 'Whether the Holy Ghost be *given*'—exactly as the same words are translated in John vii. 39.— The former part of this verse may be compared with what was said on chap. xi. 17.

Ib. 9. *That way.* τὴν ὁδόν. 'The way;' or, if it would not be thought too free, ' the religion.' 'The sect' might certainly be considered objectionable, as conveying, at least in modern language, a contemptuous idea.—I do not think our Translators have happily got over the difficulty of this expression by rendering *this way, that way.* Compare chap. ix. 2, xxiv. 22, and ver. 23 of the present chapter; and see above on Matt. xv. 12. The term appears singular to us; but we must go back for it to the Old Testament, where it occurs in Psalm lxvii. 2, *that thy way may be known upon earth;* a passage, which I regret that the venerable Compilers of our Liturgy have in some measure perverted in the beautiful prayer for all conditions of men, *that thou wouldst be pleased to make thy* WAYS *known unto them.*—Perhaps ·if our Translators had in the first instance adhered to the literal rendering, *the way*, the apparent quaintness of it would long since have worn off.

Ib. 13. *Of the vagabond Jews, exorcists.* τῶν περιερχομένων Ἰουδαίων ἐξορκιστῶν. 'Of the Jewish exorcists who went about *from place to place.*' Perhaps, however, the latter words *need not* be printed in Italics.

Ib. 15. *Jesus I know, and Paul I know.* τὸν Ἰησοῦν γινώσκω, καὶ τὸν Παῦλον ἐπίσταμαι. 'Jesus I acknowledge, and Paul I know.' He acknowledged the power of Jesus, and knew Paul as commissioned with that power.

Ib. 24. *Silver shrines for Diana.* ναοὺς ἀργυροῦς Ἀρτεμίδος. 'Silver shrines of Diana;' or rather, 'shrines of Diana in silver'—silver models of them.

Ib. 33. *And they drew Alexander out of the multitude, the Jews putting him forward.* ἐκ δὲ τοῦ ὄχλου προεβίβασαν Ἀλέξανδρον, προβαλλόντων αὐτὸν τῶν Ἰουδαίων. 'And they thrust Alexander forth from the multitude, the Jews pushing him forward.' Whatever be the exact meaning of this obscure passage, one thing at least is clear, that *drew out* must be a wrong translation of προεβίβασαν. It seems probable that the Jews joined with others in the action described by this word, a partial repetition of which is presented in the following clause in order to particularize and give prominence to their part in the transaction. And it would perhaps be better to hazard a slight inelegance for the sake of greater perspicuity, by repeating the word *forward; thrust forward, pushing forward.*

Ib. 39. *In a lawful assembly.* ἐν τῇ ἐννόμῳ ἐκκλησίᾳ. 'In the regular assembly.'

xxi. 4. *And finding disciples.* καὶ ἀνευρόντες τοὺς μαθητάς. 'And having found out the disciples.' The article recognises the existence of these disciples, and assumes the previous knowledge of that existence. Hence they were led to search for them: whereas the other translation would imply that they found unexpectedly and by accident, that there were disciples in the place.

Ib. 15. *We took up our carriages.* ἀποσκευασάμενοι, or ἐπισκ. 'We put up our baggage.'

Ib. 38. *Art not thou*—οὐκ ἄρα σὺ εἶ—'Art thou not then'—

Ib. 39. *I am a man* which am *a Jew of Tarsus,* a city *in Cilicia.* ἐγὼ ἄνθρωπος μέν εἰμι Ἰουδαῖος Ταρσεὺς τῆς Κιλικίας. 'I am a Jew of Tarsus in Cilicia.' The same correction should be applied to v. 3 of the next chapter. In both instances the common translation is quite encumbered with a weight of words, producing a tedious repetition: *I am—which am—city—citizen—city.*

xxii. 23. *And cast off* their *clothes.* καὶ ῥιπτούντων τὰ ἱμάτια. 'And threw up their garments:' not *cast them off,* but holding their loose garments in their hands shook them and tossed them upward.

xxiii. 27. *Should have been killed.* μέλλοντα ἀναιρεῖσθαι. 'Was on the point of being killed.'

Ibid. *With an army.* σὺν τῷ στρατεύματι. 'With my soldiers.'

xxiv. 22. *I will know the uttermost of your matter.* διαγνώσομαι τὰ καθ' ὑμᾶς. 'I will judge of the matters between you.' Compare διάγνωσιν in chap. xxv. 21.

Ib. 23. *A centurion.* τῷ ἑκατοντάρχῃ. 'The centurion.'
All the difficulty of the expression, which is just such as
to mark that conscious clearness in the Historian which
nothing but truth could give, is solved by Bishop Middleton with his usual accuracy of investigation.   Of the two
centurions, who had been sent with Paul from Jerusalem,
the one had left him at Antipatris (xxiii. 32), the other
proceeded with him to Cesarea: he therefore is THE centurion here mentioned.

xxv. 5. *If there be any* wickedness *in him.*   εἴ τι ἔστιν
ἐν τῷ ἀνδρὶ τούτῳ. 'Whatever *fault* there be in him.' See
the notes on Rom. xiii. 9, and Philipp. iv. 8.

xxvi. 18. And *to turn* them. τοῦ ἐπιστρέψαι. 'That
they may turn.' The τοῦ ἐπιστρέψαι is not in the same
construction with the preceding ἀνοῖξαι, to *open,* but with
the following τοῦ λαβεῖν, which is properly rendered, *that
they may receive.* And though ἐπιστρέψαι is strictly speaking a transitive verb, yet its *general* usage in the New
Testament, which has also the sanction of classical writers,
is intransitive. See v. 20 of this chapter, Luke xxii. 32.
Acts iii. 19. Soph. Trachin. 566.

Ib. 23. And *that he should be the first that should rise
from the dead, and should shew light.* εἰ πρῶτος ἐξ ἀναστάσεως νεκρῶν φῶς μέλλει καταγγέλλειν. '*And* that he first
by *his* resurrection from the dead should shew light.'
This is in more exact conformity with the original, and
also marks more clearly the reference, which I doubt not
is contained in the passage, to Psalm cxviii. 27, as a striking
prediction of the resurrection.

xxvii. 12. *And lieth.* βλέποντα. 'Looking.' Our Translators appear to me to have been doubly unfortunate here.
In the first place, it is much better to retain the participle
than to change it into a verb with a copula, as the word
has nothing emphatic in it, but is merely descriptive of
situation. In the next place, the word they have chosen
seems very inappropriate: it leads us to expect that the
Historian is about to explain in what part of the island
this harbour is situated, and then we must needs be
puzzled to know what middle point it is between the S.W.
and N.W.; whereas in fact the word describes only the
aspect of it.

Ib. 15. *Bear up into the wind.* ἀντοφθαλμεῖν τῷ ἀνέμῳ.
'Bear up against the wind.'

Ib. 40. *And when they had taken up the anchors, they
committed* themselves *unto the sea.* καὶ τὰς ἀγκύρας περιε-
λόντες εἴων εἰς τὴν θάλασσαν. 'And having cut the anchors
they let *them* go into the sea:' nearly as in the margin.
I can hardly agree with Dr. Doddridge, that the original
here is dubious. In v. 20. περιῃρεῖτο is used in a sense
very nearly similar.

Ib. 44. *And some on* broken pieces *of the ship.* οὓς
δὲ ἐπί τινων ἀπὸ τοῦ πλοίου. 'And others on some of the
things from the ship.' For what were the *boards*, or *planks*,
but *broken pieces of the ship?* τὰ ἀπὸ πλοίου therefore must
mean the articles with which the ship was laden, which
were thrown out for the purpose, or scattered by the
violence of the tempest.

4

ST. PAUL'S EPISTLE TO THE ROMANS.

CHAP. i. 17. *For therein is the righteousness of God revealed from faith to faith.* δικαιοσύνη γὰρ Θεοῦ ἐν αὐτῷ ἀποκαλύπτεται ἐκ πίστεως εἰς πίστιν. 'For therein is the righteousness of God revealed, *being* by faith, unto faith.' I understand εἰς πίστιν to be equivalent to εἰς τὸ πιστεῦσαι ἡμᾶς, to the end that we may believe, or may receive it by faith. This use of the preposition εἰς, as marking the end of an action or thing, is very common with St. Paul, especially in this epistle: compare ver. 5 of this chapter, and chap. vi. 16, 19. viii. 15. x. 10. xiii. 4, 14. From a comparison of these passages, and of the form adopted in the translation of the last of them, we may perhaps feel warranted in admitting a somewhat greater latitude in rendering the present passage, confessedly a difficult one—'that we may believe,' or 'may have faith *in it.*' So in chap. vi. 16, δούλους εἰς ὑπακοὴν, *servants for obedience, servants to obey,* i. e. that ye may obey.

The passage will receive additional light, and I think the view here taken of it some confirmation, by a comparison with the fuller statement of the very same thing in chap. iii. 21, 22, where the apostle resumes the subject after a long digression in which he had argued the need of this gospel-remedy both to Gentiles and Jews. The reader will observe, that δικαιοσύνη Θεοῦ ἐν αὐτῷ ἀποκαλύπτεται of the first chapter answers to νυνὶ δὲ χωρὶς νόμου ὁ δικαιοσύνη Θεοῦ πεφανέρωται of the third: again, ἐκ πίστεως of the former to δικαιοσύνη δὲ Θεοῦ διὰ πίστεως Ἰησοῦ Χριστοῦ of the latter; and εἰς πίστιν to εἰς πάντας καὶ ἐπὶ πάντας τοὺς πιστεύοντας. This comparison seems to me also to establish the substantial identity of the two phrases ἐκ πίστεως and διὰ πίστεως in regard to justification. See chap. iii. 30, and many other passages.

I need scarcely add, that I reject as entirely unsatisfactory the two more popular methods of interpreting the passage—that it is altogether by faith, or proceeding from one degree of faith to another. Lightfoot's view is a modification of this latter,—that it is from the faith of the law to the faith of the Gospel, from faith in God to faith in Christ.

Ib. 26. *For even their women.* αἵ τε γὰρ θήλειαι αὐτῶν. 'For both their women'—followed by, *Likewise also the men*, in v. 27.

iii. 4. *And mightest overcome when thou art judged.* καὶ νικήσῃς ἐν τῷ κρίνεσθαί σε. 'And mightest overcome when thou standest in judgment.' The Bible translation (Psalm li. 4) is, *when thou judgest;* and the Apostle's quotation is made exactly from the Septuagint: in which it appears more natural, and more in accordance with the original, to understand κρίνεσθαι as a middle verb, of which the proper force is, not to judge another, or to be judged by another, but to stand in judgment, or go to law, with another. 1 Corinth. vi. 1, κρίνεσθαι ἐπὶ τῶν ἀδίκων. So Eurip. Medea, 609, ὡς οὐ κρινοῦμαι τῶνδέ σοι τὰ πλείονα. *I will not dispute.*

iv. 24. *If we believe.* τοῖς πιστεύουσιν. 'Who believe.'
This is clearly the sense of the words, though there is
some awkwardness in expressing it on account of the
clause interposed, οἷς μέλλει λογίζεσθαι.

v. 3. *We glory.* καυχώμεθα. 'We rejoice.' The Apostle
has three declarations strictly connected together, however
separated by space. In v. 2, *we rejoice in hope;* in v. 3,
we rejoice in tribulations; in v. 11, *we rejoice in God.* In
all these cases the original word is the same, καυχώμεθα,
though in the last in the form of a participle; yet our
Translators have varied it in each case, *rejoice, glory, joy.*
This is surely not conveying to an English reader the
most correct idea that might be conveyed of the spirit of
the original.

Ib. 7. *For scarcely for a righteous man will one die:*
yet peradventure for a good man some would even dare to
die. μόλις γὰρ ὑπὲρ δικαίου τὶς ἀποθανεῖται· ὑπὲρ γὰρ τοῦ
ἀγαθοῦ τάχα τὶς καὶ τολμᾷ ἀποθανεῖν. 'For scarcely will
one die for a righteous man : *I say, scarcely;* for perhaps
for a good man one would dare even to die.' I can propose nothing on this passage that is not vague and uncertain ; and I find nothing in others to help me through
the difficulty. It is remarkable that Bishop Middleton
takes no notice of the Article before ἀγαθοῦ, though to
me it appears to increase the difficulty not a little. It
is, I think, evident that the Apostle intended the latter
clause to qualify the former; in which if he had made
his statement too exclusive, he would be willing so far
to recede from it as to allow that for a righteous and good

man some might possibly be found willing to die; but still it furnished no parallel to the love of God. I consider the ἀγαθοῦ therefore as not essentially different from the δικαίου, but expressing *the same* character by a more general term, with perhaps the Article added for the sake of emphasis.

I have translated as above on the principle, that where two successive clauses are commenced with γὰρ, the latter γὰρ has either the force of *verily,* as in chap. xv. 27 of this Epistle; or else marks something elliptical, which I have supposed to be the case here.

May I venture to propose another rendering of the latter clause? ' Perhaps indeed for a good man one would dare even to die: but God—' Something like this, I think, is the complexion which γὰρ gives to a sentence in Thucydides I. 142, fin. πρὸς μὲν γὰρ ὀλίγας ἐφορμούσας κἂν διακινδυνεύσειαν. *against a few indeed they might hazard—*

Ib. 12. *Have sinned.* ἥμαρτον. ' Sinned.' The other form appears to me to violate not only the literal correctness, but the strictness of the argument.

Ib. 13. *For until the law.* ἄχρι γὰρ νόμου. ' For during the law,' or, ' during *the time of* the law.' In the other translation, *until the law* in the sense of *before the law* is unsatisfactory and obscure: its natural meaning would be, that sin was in the world until the law came, but no longer—manifestly against the mind of the writer. In the proposed translation the reasoning is as follows: Death passed upon all men, because sin extended to all—

death and sin were co-extensive. Death therefore did not exist without sin: *for*—(he stops to anticipate an objection)—it is an agreed principle, and no one wonders, that death existed under and during the law, because *sin was in the world; but* how does it hold in regard to the times before the law? for *sin is not imputed where there is no law:* how then could there be death antecedently to the law? *Nevertheless,* says the apostle, during the whole interval *from Adam to Moses death reigned;* and therefore there must have been sin—πάντες ἥμαρτον, v. 12. And so it falls in with his general argument.

Ib. 20. *Moreover the law entered.* νόμος δὲ παρεισῆλθεν. 'And the law entered incidentally.' I am aware that this expression will hardly suit the general simplicity of style which so admirably characterises our authorised translation; but it is better than another, which is perhaps still more correct, *entered by the by.* Our Translators seem to have intended to express the παρὰ by *moreover.* Bishop Middleton objects to παρεισῆλθεν being applied to the law of Moses, because that, instead of *entering privily,* came in with much pomp and notoriety. But I consider the sense of it to be, that when sin had entered, the direct and obvious method would have been to introduce the gospel as its great counteraction and remedy; instead of which the law came first to answer a collateral end, viz. to aggravate the evil and make it more manifest and desperate, that men might be most effectually prepared to welcome the blessing. Thus it was an *indirect* step towards the accomplishment of God's ultimate purpose.

vi. 17. *But God be thanked that ye were the servants of sin, but ye have obeyed.* χάρις δὲ τῷ Θεῷ ὅτι ἦτε δοῦλοι τῆς ἁμαρτίας, ὑπηκούσατε δέ. 'But God be thanked, that, whereas ye were servants of sin, ye have obeyed.' That this exhibits the spirit of the passage, cannot be doubted. The literal rendering adopted by our Translators represents the Apostle as thanking God as well for their former state of bondage, as for their recovery from it: whereas his real object in mentioning the bondage is only to magnify by contrast the grace of the deliverance. A passage exactly similar in construction (except that the order of the clauses is inverted) occurs in 2 Cor. xiii. 7, where our Translators have not hesitated to use the freedom of alteration here recommended: ἵνα ὑμεῖς τὸ καλὸν ποιῆτε, ἡμεῖς δὲ ὡς ἀδόκιμοι ὦμεν. *That ye should do that which is honest,* THOUGH *we be as reprobates.* Compare also Matthew xi. 25.

viii. 1. There is *therefore now no condemnation to them which are in Christ Jesus, who walk not after the flesh, but after the Spirit.* οὐδὲν ἄρα νῦν κατάκριμα τοῖς ἐν Χριστῷ Ἰησοῦ μὴ κατὰ σάρκα περιπατοῦσιν, ἀλλὰ κατὰ πνεῦμα. 'Now then *there is* no condemnation to those, who in Christ Jesus walk not after the flesh, but after the Spirit.' I do not consider the statement of this verse so direct a conclusion from the preceding argument, as the word *therefore* would represent it to be. Nor yet do I agree with Dr. Doddridge in thinking that the chapters are here unhappily divided, and that the ἄρα νῦν of this verse and the ἄρα οὖν of the preceding answer to each other in the way which he supposes. Still less can I agree with those who, to uphold particular views of doctrine of one kind or another, separate this chapter entirely from the seventh, and connect it with the sixth, throwing the whole seventh chapter into an imaginary parenthesis. The connexion appears to me to be clear and forcible, and the division of the chapters to be made just where it ought to be.

The concluding words of chap. vii. *So then with the mind,* &c. contain a kind of summing up of the Apostle's whole statement of his condition and experience as a believer. That condition in some points appeared to be so nearly hopeless, that it might lead to the suspicion that such a person could not be in a converted state at all: but in opposition to this the Apostle concludes, *I myself,* sinful as I am, *serve with the mind the law of God, but with the flesh the law of sin.* The character in question being thus settled to be that of a spiritual man, another conclusion might seem to be reasonably drawn from the whole statement, which would open out a quite different part of the subject, viz. that a person described as so much under the power of corruption must be in a state of condemnation. This the Apostle takes up and replies to in the former part of the present chapter, in which he does not argue *the way of justification,* but maintains the connexion of justification and sanctification, and the certainty of salvation to those who, like himself, *walk not after the flesh, but after the Spirit. There is no condemnation to* them; and the ground of their deliverance, as well as the principle of their sanctification, is just alluded to in the words, *in Christ Jesus*. This view is borne out by the arrangement here adopted, which includes the whole description of character in one clause; nor do I see how the other arrangement can be admitted without the repetition of the article τοῖς before περιπατοῦσιν.

Ib. 3. *And for sin.* καὶ περὶ ἁμαρτίας. 'And *as a sacrifice* for sin.' Compare Hebrews x. 6, 8.

Ib. 10. *The body* is *dead.* τὸ μὲν σῶμα νεκρόν. 'The body indeed *is* dead.' The common translation makes the deadness of the body to follow as a consequence of Christ being in us: and this might in a certain sense be admitted; but then the other consequence, viz. that *the Spirit is life,* must be connected with it by the copula *and,* and not by the adversative *but.* The new rendering makes the former clause a kind of concession, q. d. I grant that *the body* is still dead, and so far the redemption is incomplete (compare v. 23); *but the Spirit,* &c.

Ib. 11. *But if the Spirit.* εἰ δὲ τὸ πνεῦμα. 'And if the Spirit.' This verse contains little more than an amplification of the statement of v. 10, both being introduced with the same particles εἰ δέ. The variation in the translation interferes with the clearness of the Apostle's reasoning.

Ib. ib. *By his Spirit that dwelleth in you.* διὰ τὸ ἐνοικοῦν αὐτοῦ πνεῦμα ἐν ὑμῖν. 'Because of his Spirit that dwelleth in you'—as in the margin. There are in fact two readings in the original, that quoted above, and διὰ τοῦ ἐνοικοῦντος αὐτοῦ πνεύματος. This latter is the reading of the received text, which our Translators followed: what they have given in the margin was not intended to be a different translation, but a translation of a different original, which is followed by Griesbach; and both on the ground of authority and suitableness to the sense this appears to be much preferable to the other.

Ib. 19. *Of the creature.* τῆς κτίσεως. 'Of the creation.' So it is translated in v. 22, and for the sake of clearness and uniformity the same translation should be adopted in this verse and the two following.

Ib. 23. *Waiting for the adoption,* to wit, *the redemption of our body.* υἱοθεσίαν ἀπεκδεχόμενοι τὴν ἀπολύτρωσιν τοῦ σώματος ἡμῶν. 'Waiting for the redemption of our body as the adoption.' The two accusatives following the participle in apposition with one another, the one having the Article prefixed and the other not, make it clear that ἀπολύτρωσιν is the object, to which υἱοθεσίαν is subjoined as its explanation. *As the adoption,* as the completion or declaration of our adoption.

ix. 18. *Therefore hath he mercy.* ἄρα οὖν... ἐλεεῖ. 'So then he hath mercy.' If *therefore* be retained, it would mark the conclusion from a foregoing argument; whereas the quotations in the preceding verses are brought forward only in illustration.

Ib. 22. What *if God, willing.* εἰ δὲ θέλων ὁ Θεός. 'And if God, willing.' If the common translation be retained, the insertion of *what* may be justified by John vi. 62; and the only objection to its adoption here is, that it is unnecessary. The passage appears to me to be an immediate application of the comparison in the preceding verse of the potter and the clay; and the sentence is completed in v. 30, the intermediate verses, 25—29, being in a parenthesis. The analogy between the two cases is complete. The potter, v. 21, has power to make one vessel to honour, another to dishonour: so God, v. 22—3, has the same power with regard to the vessels of wrath and the vessels of mercy. The thing formed, πλάσμα, v. 20, cannot reply against the former of it: neither can we against God, v. 30. Compare μὴ ἐρεῖ τὸ πλάσμα, and τί οὖν ἐροῦμεν;

In v. 23 the construction is defective. The Apostle seems to have supplied in his mind from the preceding verse *endured with much long-suffering,* or, *exercised the same long-suffering*—intimating that both classes deserved condemnation, and therefore needed the long-suffering of God, but that in the one case that *long-suffering* was *salvation,* and not in the other.

Ib. 27. *Esaias also crieth.* Ἡσαΐας δὲ κράζει. 'But Esaias crieth.' The quotation from Hosea having affirmed the calling of the Gentiles into the church, this from Isaiah seems to be added to account for the exclusion of a large portion of Israel.

xi. 32. *For God hath concluded them all.* συνέκλεισε γὰρ ὁ Θεὸς τοὺς πάντας. 'For God hath concluded all.' The insertion of *them* restricts it to the Jews; whereas the argument requires it to mean *all,* both Jews and Gentiles.

xii. 3. *Not to think* of himself *more highly than he ought to think, but to think soberly.* μὴ ὑπερφρονεῖν παρ' ὃ δεῖ φρονεῖν, ἀλλὰ φρονεῖν εἰς τὸ σωφρονεῖν. 'Not to be wise above what he ought to be, but to be wise unto sobriety.' This sense of φρονεῖν here is adopted by Archbishop Usher (*Religion of the ancient Irish*, chap. i. init.); and the scope of the passage, compared with 1 Corinth. iv. 6, (where see) seems to require it rather than the other; which indeed is at best a doubtful one, requiring in both passages, if admitted, a very awkward supplement for completing the sentence—*of himself, of men.*

xiii. 9. *For this, Thou shalt not commit adultery, ... Thou shalt not covet; and if* there be *any other commandment, it is briefly comprehended in this saying.* τὸ γάρ· Οὐ μοιχεύσεις· . . . . Οὐκ ἐπιθυμήσεις· καὶ εἴ τις ἑτέρα ἐντολὴ, ἐν τούτῳ τῷ λόγῳ ἀνακεφαλαιοῦται. 'For the *commandment,* Thou shalt not commit adultery, . . . Thou shalt not covet, and whatever other commandment *there is,* it is summed up in this saying.' In other words, the command not to commit adultery, &c. and all the others are summed up in this. The expression, *For this,* at the beginning of the common translation, is apt to mislead the Reader; and the *too literal* rendering of εἴ τις adds to the perplexity. See on Philipp. iv. 8.

Ib. 11. *And that, knowing the time.* καὶ τοῦτο, εἰδότες τὸν καιρόν. 'And this *do as* knowing the time.'

xiv. 4. *Another man's servant.* ἀλλότριον οἰκέτην. 'Another's servant'—i. e. God's; as in the close of the verse. See on Luke xvi. 12.

Ib. *Yea, he shall be holden up.* σταθήσεται δέ. 'And he shall be made to stand.' One idea runs through the verse, στήκει, σταθήσεται, στῆσαι. To *stand* in judgment, i.e. to be accepted. Thou condemnest, who art not his master; but God, who is, accepts him (προσελάβετο, v. 3,) and will make him stand.

Ib. 23. *Is damned if he eat, because* he eateth *not of faith.* ἐὰν φάγῃ, κατακέκριται, ὅτι οὐκ ἐκ πίστεως. 'Is con-demned if he eat, because *it is* not of faith.' The former change is necessary only on account of the change which our language has undergone; the latter is made for the greater simplicity.

xv. 6.   See below, on 1 Pet. i. 3.

Ib. 12. *In him shall the Gentiles trust.* ἐπ' αὐτῷ ἔθνη ἐλπιοῦσιν. 'In him shall the Gentiles hope.' The change is made simply because it immediately follows, *Now the God of hope,* τῆς ἐλπίδος. It is as if the Apostle had meant to follow up the quotation with a comment to this effect: 'And I pray that this blessing promised to the Gentiles may be abundantly fulfilled to you Gentiles.'

Ib. 20. *Yea, so have I strived to preach the gospel.* οὕτω δὲ φιλοτιμούμενον εὐαγγελίζεσθαι. 'Yet so striving to preach it.' The connexion of this verse with the preceding passage by *Yea* does not accord with the simplicity of the original; and the more literal rendering of δὲ, *but* or *yet,* enforces with great clearness the subject of the Apostle's glorying, vv. 16—8. Instead of repeating the term, *the gospel,* which is done for an obvious reason in the ori-ginal, it is better in English to substitute the pronoun.

xvi. 9. *Urbane.* Οὐρβανόν. 'Urbanus.' Urbane is liable to be mistaken for the name of a female.

Ib. 23. *Quartus a brother.* Κούαρτος ὁ ἀδελφός. 'Quartus the brother.' If Quartus had been only *a* brother, one unknown to the Romans, why should he salute them?

THE FIRST EPISTLE TO THE CORINTHIANS.

CHAP. i. 4, 5. *By Jesus Christ; by him.* ἐν Χριστῷ Ἰησοῦ ἐν αὐτῷ. 'In Jesus Christ; in him.' There is no sufficient reason for varying from the original. Compare Ephesians i. 3, *With all spiritual blessings* . . . IN CHRIST.

Ib. 10, 12. *Now I beseech you. Now this I say.* παρακαλῶ δὲ ὑμᾶς. λέγω δὲ τοῦτο. 'But I beseech you.' 'And this I mean.' In both these verses, as in Chap. iii. 12, the rendering *now* for δέ seems to be very injurious to the sense and scope of the apostle.

In ver. 10, the connexion with the preceding verses is quite obscured. Having expressed his thankfulness (v. 4) for the grace of God bestowed on the Corinthians, and then (vv. 8, 9) his confidence in the continuance of that grace, St. Paul proceeds to guard them by suitable warnings against serious dangers they were exposed to. BUT— with this confidence in reference to God, I have anxious misgivings with regard to yourselves; and therefore—*I beseech you* to beware of divisions, &c. &c.

In ver. 12, according to the common translation, we should expect that the Apostle was about to open some new matter of complaint; whereas he merely proceeds to explain the nature of the ἔριδες mentioned in v. 11.

ii. 15. *Judgeth, is judged.* ἀνακρίνει, ἀνακρίνεται. 'Discerneth, is discerned'—as in the margin, and in the preceding verse.

iii. 12. *Now if any man.* εἰ δέ τις. 'But if any man.' The common translation, whatever may have been the reason for adopting it, injures the perspicuity of the argument, which requires an opposition between this verse and the preceding. The Apostle speaks of himself as having laid the foundation of the Corinthian church by preaching Christ to them; and then cautions the other teachers how they built on the foundation thus laid. For, says he, as to the foundation itself, I have no fear about that—*no man can lay* any *other,* and you are too well taught to endure any other, *than that* which *is laid* already, *which is Christ Jesus: but* with regard to those who *build upon* this foundation, the teachers who come into the church thus planted, *if any man build,* &c.

Ib. 15. *By fire.* διὰ πυρός. 'Through fire'—having been himself in a degree of jeopardy, from which he has scarcely escaped. Eurip. Electr. 1182, διὰ πυρὸς ἔμολον ἁ τάλαινα μητρὶ τᾷδ'. See the note on 1 Peter iii. 20.

Ib. 17. *If any man defile the temple of God.* εἴ τις τὸν ναὸν τοῦ Θεοῦ φθείρει. 'If any man destroy the temple of God,' as in the margin. The φθείρει and φθερεῖ are evidently opposed to each other in the same sense. And *the temple of God,* which is the church, is not so much *defiled,* as *destroyed* and overthrown, by false doctrine.

iv. 6. *Not to think* of men *above that which is written.* τὸ μὴ ὑπὲρ ὃ γέγραπται φρονεῖν. 'Not to be wise above that which is written.' See on Rom. xii. 3. Even if φρονεῖν, used by itself, could bear the sense assigned to it in the common translation, *to think of men*, it would not be easy to understand how that sense could suit the passage. With regard to the question, whether the Apostle's ad-monition is directed to the false teachers or their disciples, the words immediately following in this verse seem to make it clear, that however the former may be glanced at, the direct address is exclusively to the latter. Why then are they cautioned against the conceit of superior wisdom? Just because it was the arrogant pretension to such superior wisdom which led them to despise "the old ways" of the Apostle's teaching, and to "glory" in their false apostles. Hence he speaks of their being *puffed up for one against another;* and in the preceding chapter, vv. 18, seqq. the censure of vain and conceited pretension to wisdom appears to be directed at least as much against the disciples of error as against their se-ducers.

Ib. 9. *Unto the world, and to angels, and to men.* τῷ κόσμῳ καὶ ἀγγέλοις καὶ ἀνθρώποις. 'Unto the world, both angels and men.' This correction is anticipated by Dod-dridge, and perhaps by others; and, independently of the sense, the absence of the articles before ἀγγέλοις and ἀνθρώποις might lead us to adopt it. See Bp. Middleton in loc.

Ib. 17. *My ways which be in Christ.* τὰς ὁδούς μου τὰς

ἐν Χριστῷ. 'My ways in Christ.' The second τὰς is added merely to define the ways mentioned, and need not be expressed in English. It might have been either τὰς ἐν Χριστῷ ὁδούς μου, or τὰς ὁδούς μου τὰς ἐν Χ.; just as, if an adjective had been employed, e. g. εὐθείας, the form would have been either τὰς εὐθείας ὁδοὺς, or τὰς ὁδοὺς τὰς εὐθείας. The spirit of this remark might also be applied to 1 Timothy i. 4, 14.

v. 1. *Is not so much as named among the Gentiles.* οὐδὲ ἐν τοῖς ἔθνεσιν ὀνομάζεται. 'Is not named even among the Gentiles.'

Ib. 9. *I wrote unto you in an epistle.* ἔγραψα ὑμῖν ἐν τῇ ἐπιστολῇ. 'I have written unto you in my epistle.' I entirely acquiesce in the opinion so ably stated by Bishop Middleton, that the Apostle is speaking of his present epistle, not of a former one. Ἔγραψα, both in the 9th and 11th verses, might be rendered, I think, with equal accuracy, *I write;* but at all events it must be rendered the same way in both verses, and that must be, not *I wrote,* but *I have written,* or *I write.* The Greek and Latin writers, more accurately than ourselves perhaps, express this action in a past tense, because it will be a past action when it is presented to the mind of the reader. So Thucydides ɪ. 23, prop. fin. says, προέγραψα πρῶτον, what he is going to write immediately after; and what we express, *I write this from Rome,* is *Dabam Romæ.*— But there is a further difficulty in the νυνὶ of v. 11, which seems to be opposed to what he had written before. But I conceive that the word is not there used in reference to

5

time; but in a sense similar to the very common one in which it occurs in Hebrews xi. 16, νυνὶ δὲ κρείττονος ὀρέγονται, with which compare Demosth. de Cor. p. 271, 20, νῦν δὲ ὑμεῖς στρεβλώσαντες, etc. where, instead of meaning *at this present time*, it means evidently *as the case really turned out*: and a similar interpretation is given of the word by Professor Dobree in his Adversaria, vol. I. p. 28, on Herodot. II. 146. Upon this principle νυνὶ δὲ ἔγραψα will signify, *But what I really mean by writing thus, is*—so that it will be an explanation of, and not an opposition to, the ἔγραψα of v. 9. Compare Philem. 19, 21.

vi. 15. *Shall I then take the members of Christ, and make them*—ἄρας οὖν τὰ μέλη τοῦ Χριστοῦ ποιήσω—'Shall I then make the members of Christ'—For ἄρας Valckenær adopts the reading of many MSS. ἄρα. The common translation does not read amiss in the English, but the ἄρας in the Greek is certainly uncouth.

vii. 11. *But and if she depart.* ἐὰν δὲ καὶ χωρισθῇ. 'But if also she be separated.' The same with χωρισθῆναι in the preceding verse. I suppose our Translators intended *depart* here in its old sense for *part;* of which usage there is, I believe, a remnant, now obliterated, in our marriage-service: *till death us do part.* Qu. *depart?*—See however the authorised translation of Philem. 15.

Ib. 13. *And if he be pleased to dwell with her, let her not leave him.* καὶ αὐτὸς συνευδοκεῖ οἰκεῖν μετ' αὐτῆς, μὴ ἀφιέτω αὐτόν. 'If he be pleased to dwell with her, let her not put him away.' Ἀφιέτω is the same word that is used in the two preceding verses, and there is no objection to retaining the same translation. In the former clause our Translators have inserted *if* in order to adhere in a manner to a construction which has a little harshness in the original, but can hardly be retained in our language. I have endeavoured to obviate the difficulty by changing *and* into *if*. Both clauses in fact contain an hypothesis: If a woman have an unbelieving husband, and if he be pleased to dwell with her. But in the former clause the hypothesis is put in a different form, *the woman* WHICH *hath,* etc.; and as the relative *which* cannot be the nominative of the second clause, the other form of hypothesis must be introduced, which can only be done by changing *and* into *if*.

viii. 8. *But meat commendeth us not to God.* Βρῶμα δὲ ἡμᾶς οὐ παρίστησι τῷ Θεῷ. 'Now meat commendeth us not to God.' The argument will hardly admit of·δὲ in the adversative sense here, especially as another δὲ follows in the next verse. The object seems to be to lay down a principle upon which the strong believer may be urged to forbearance from consideration towards his weak brother. *Now* consider that *meat commendeth us not*—either its use or disuse is a matter of indifference—you therefore can forego your liberty without any prejudice—*But,* if you use it, *take heed lest,* &c.

ix. 17. *A dispensation of the gospel is committed unto me.* οἰκονομίαν πεπίστευμαι. 'I have a stewardship committed unto me'—which therefore I must fulfil, whether willingly or not, as a matter of duty. Compare chap. iv. 1, 2.

Ib. 23. *That I might be partaker thereof with* you. ἵνα συγκοινωνὸς αὐτοῦ γένωμαι. 'That I may be a partaker with it'—i.e. a sharer in those triumphs which it accomplishes in the conversion and salvation of sinners by my instrumentality. It is altogether a mistake to suppose that in such a construction the dative is necessarily required instead of the genitive: compare Romans viii. 17. 1 Corinth. iii. 9 (with which 2 Cor. vi. 1.) Ephes. ii. 19. Revel. xix. 10, &c. and in classical writers, to take one example out of many, Herodot. ii. 134, σύνδουλος Αἰσώπου.

Ib. 25. See on 2 Tim. ii. 5.

x. 5. *But with many of them.* ἀλλ᾽ . . . . ἐν τοῖς πλείοσιν αὐτῶν. 'But with the most of them.'

Ib. 17. *For we* being *many are one bread,* and *one body.* ὅτι εἷς ἄρτος, ἓν σῶμα οἱ πολλοί ἐσμεν. 'For *there is* one bread, *and* we who are many are one body.' The common translation must be discarded as scarcely intelligible. The proposed correction contains two distinct propositions, but so connected together as to indicate comparison: As *there is one bread,* so *we,* &c. This form of comparison is frequent in the *Proverbs* and elsewhere. Ex. gr. Prov. xx. 30, literally, *and stripes,* &c. Some would accordingly render here, *As* there is one bread, *So* we—which makes the sense more clear, and is only objectionable (if at all) as being less literal. Dr. Waterland (*Review of the Doctrine of the Eucharist,* chap. viii. init.) reads it, *For since the bread is one, we being many are one body.* Thus he says the passage is "correctly rendered, as near as may be to the Greek original." Did he mean ὅτι to include the two particles, *for* and *since?* Doubtless it might ex-press either of them, but cannot include both.

Ib. 29. *But of the other.* ἀλλὰ τὴν τοῦ ἑτέρου. 'But that of the other.' In the common translation τὴν is omitted. In the early editions it is printed ' of the others.' Did our Translators intend to print it, ' but the other's?' The apostrophe in such cases is usually omitted by them.

xi. 23. *For I have received.* ἐγὼ γὰρ παρέλαβον. 'For I received.' It is clear that the sense is injured by the deviation from the proper tense.

Ib. 27. *And drink.* ἢ πίνῃ. ' Or drink.' Some copies however read καὶ πίνῃ. But it was hardly worth while for the Roman Catholic translators to subjoin the following annotation: "Here erroneous translators corrupted the text by putting *and drink* (contrary to the original, ἢ πίνῃ) instead of *or drink.*" For while the bread *and* cup are joined together in vv. 26, 28, and 29, what force can there be in the use of the disjunctive *or* once, in v. 27, to jus-tify their withholding the cup from the laity?

xii. 2. *Unto these dumb idols.* πρὸς τὰ εἴδωλα τὰ ἄφωνα. ' Unto dumb idols.' If *these,* what? and if it be asked, what is the force of the Articles according to the new translation? I answer, they are properly inserted to de-note a *class*—idols in general. See Middleton, p. 57. Part I. ch. III. sect. II. § 2.

xiv. 25. *In you.* ἐν ὑμῖν. ' Among you.'.

Ib. 29. *Let the other judge.* οἱ ἄλλοι διακρινέτωσαν. ' Let the rest judge.' The word *other* may be mistaken for the singular number, and so create obscurity.

Ib. 33. *God is not* the author *of confusion.* οὐ γάρ
ἐστιν ἀκαταστασίας ὁ Θεός. 'God is not *the God* of confusion.' The form of the sentence is similar to Luke xx.
38, Θεὸς οὐκ ἔστι νεκρῶν, and it seems better to repeat
Θεὸς before ἀκαταστασίας, than to *supply* another word.

xv. 1, 2. To say, as it is in our translation, *I declare
unto you the gospel which I preached unto you,* seems to be
an assertion little better than gratuitous. The construction of the passage, by mistaking which our Translators
have made strange confusion in v. 2, is well explained by
Professor Dobree, Advers. vol. I. p. 571: γνωρίζω τὸ εὐαγγέλιον τίνι λόγῳ εὐηγγελισάμην—a common Greek idiom
for γνωρίζω τίνι λόγῳ εὐηγγελισάμην τὸ εὐαγγέλιον. With
this he properly compares Galat. i. 11. According to this
view the Greek must be printed as follows:

Γνωρίζω δὲ ὑμῖν, ἀδελφοὶ, τὸ εὐαγγέλιον ὃ εὐηγγελισάμην
ὑμῖν, (ὃ καὶ παρελάβετε, ἐν ᾧ καὶ ἑστήκατε, δι' οὗ καὶ σώζεσθε,)
τίνι λόγῳ εὐηγγελισάμην ὑμῖν, εἰ κατέχετε, ἐκτὸς εἰ μὴ εἰκῇ
ἐπιστεύσατε.

'Moreover, brethren, I certify you *concerning* the
gospel which I preached unto you, (which also ye received,
and wherein ye stand, and by which ye are saved,)

With what declaration (or, with what manner of dis-
course) I preached *it* to you, if ye remember, unless ye
believed lightly.'

Here again I think our Translators have greatly perplexed the passage by twice inserting the word *have.* Dr.
Doddridge, following the authorised translation in connecting εἰ κατέχετε with σώζεσθε, judged naturally enough

that κατέχετε should be differently translated.—In the above translation I have inserted *concerning* in the first verse, merely because in so long a sentence, and especially with the repetition of *preached* after the parenthesis, it would have been very inconvenient to take the more usual order: besides which, I could not separate εἰ κατέχετε, etc. from τίνι λόγῳ εὐηγ. ὑμῖν. I understand the λόγος, *declaration*, to refer to what follows about the great facts of Christ's death and resurrection, more especially the latter. In the concluding words the Apostle testifies that they *did* believe on his preaching, and assumes that they remembered the main topics of his preaching, unless they believed *lightly*, i. e. at random, without sufficiently attending to the things brought before them, or, as Dobree paraphrases it, *from mere caprice.*

Ib. 20. *The firstfruits of them that slept.* ἀπαρχὴ τῶν κεκοιμημένων. 'The firstfruits of them that sleep,' or 'that have fallen asleep.'

Ib. 23. *But every man in his own order.* ἕκαστος δὲ ἐν τῷ ἰδίῳ τάγματι. 'But each in his own order.' That is, as it is immediately explained, first Christ, then at a future time the people of Christ. But it does not refer to an order of succession among different *men.*

Ib. 24. *To God, even the Father.* τῷ Θεῷ καὶ πατρί. 'To God the Father.' Ὁ Θεὸς καὶ πατὴρ is a form of expression very frequently used by the Apostle to designate the first Person of the Trinity. See Coloss. ii. 2. iii. 17. Also James i. 27. iii. 9. The same expression also occurs followed by ἡμῶν, as Galat. i. 4, and frequently by τοῦ

Κυρίου Ἰησοῦ Χριστοῦ, as Romans xv. 6. 2 Corinth. i. 3. xi. 31. Ephes. i. 3. 1 Peter i. 3. In these passages our Translators have adopted different modes of rendering, where, next to accuracy, uniformity was at least desirable. A form of speech so obviously connected with a doctrine of vital importance may well be considered entitled to a brief investigation.

It is to be borne in mind that in all these examples only one Article is employed: ὁ Θεὸς καὶ πατὴρ, not καὶ ὁ πατήρ· from which the conclusion naturally follows, that only one and the same person is designated, and also that the former term Θεὸς defines his nature, and the latter πατὴρ his person. The question then is, how this may be most accurately expressed in conformity with the idiom of our language. It is clear, I think, that καὶ is to be taken as a direct copula, linking together the two parts of the designation; and therefore is not to be rendered *even*, as is sometimes done by our Translators. (See note on Coloss. ii. 2.) If again it be expressed by *and*, it either gives the appearance of *two* persons being intended (as in Coloss. iii. 17, *giving thanks to God and the Father*), or, where a genitive follows, makes it dependent on both the preceding nouns—*one God of all*, and *one Father of all* (Ephes. iv. 6. compare 1 Corinth. viii. 6,) *the God of our Lord Jesus Christ*, and *the Father of our Lord Jesus Christ*. This form of expression, *the God of our Lord Jesus Christ*, our Translators have shewn a disinclination to adopt, by occasionally substituting for it, *God even the Father*, &c. though in Ephes. i. 17 we meet with an insulated example of it.

Now, if it be agreed that the expression ὁ Θεὸς καὶ πατήρ (literally, *the God and Father*) is tantamount to, *He who is both God and the Father*, this will be accurately represented in English by, *God the Father*—whether a genitive follow, or not. Nor need it be objected, that καὶ, which is expressed in the original, is omitted in the translation, because its great use seems to be so to connect Θεὸς and πατήρ together, as to carry on the force of the Article ὁ from the one to the other; an equivalent for which is provided in the English by inserting the definite Article before the latter substantive*.

Ib. ib. *When he shall have put down all rule.* ὅταν καταργήσῃ πᾶσαν ἀρχήν. 'When he shall have destroyed all dominion.' It introduces a strange ambiguity into the passage to render καταργήσῃ here and καταργεῖται in v. 26 by different English words.

Ib. 50. *Now this I say.* τοῦτο δέ φημι. 'But this I say.' Having disposed of the case of the buried saints, the Apostle passes in the present verse to that of the living; and the translation, *Now*, makes the transition less distinct. *But*, since *flesh and blood cannot*, &c. what shall become of those who shall be found alive? They *shall be changed*, and their *corruptible* shall *put on incorruption*.

xvi. 2. *As* God *hath prospered him.* ὅ τι ἂν εὐοδῶται.

---

* Since writing the above note, I am gratified to find, that the rendering which it recommends is adopted by the venerable Tyndale in his translation, 1526.

'According as he prospereth.' Compare 3d Epistle of John, ver. 2.

Ib. 3. *Whomsoever ye shall approve by your letters, them will I send.* οὓς ἐὰν δοκιμάσητε, δι' ἐπιστολῶν τούτους πέμψω. 'Whomsoever ye shall approve, them will I send with letters.' The punctuation differs in the editions: our Translators have followed those which place the comma after ἐπιστολῶν. The other arrangement seems obviously required by the sense.

Ib. 5. *When I shall pass through Macedonia; for I do pass through Macedonia.* ὅταν Μακεδονίαν διέλθω· Μακεδονίαν γὰρ διέρχομαι. 'When I have passed through Macedonia; for I am passing through Macedonia.' One would at least suppose from the common translation, that Corinth was in Macedonia, and that St. Paul meant to visit them in his circuit through that country. I have given the exact sense of διέλθω, *when I have passed,* when I have done passing, when I have finished my circuit. Compare Demosth. Mid. p. 525, 12, ὅταν μὲν τιθῆσθε,...ἐπειδὰν δὲ θῆσθε· *when you are making, but when you* HAVE *made them—*.

If however we follow the more generally received, and apparently probable, hypothesis, that this Epistle was written from Ephesus, (see especially v. 19,) διέρχομαι must be understood in the sense of 'I am intending to pass'—as we familiarly say, I am going through such a place, for, I mean to go through.

SECOND EPISTLE TO THE CORINTHIANS.

CHAP. ii. 14. *Now thanks* be *unto God.* τῷ δὲ Θεῷ χάρις. 'But thanks *be* unto God': i. e. But though so disappointed and cast down, thanks &c.

Ib. 17. *For we are not as many, which corrupt the word of God.* (Marg. *deal deceitfully with.*) οὐ γάρ ἐσμεν ὡς οἱ πολλοὶ, (al. lect. λοιποὶ,) καπηλεύοντες τὸν λόγον τοῦ Θεοῦ. 'For we do not, like many, (or, *like most* others, or, *like the rest,*) make a traffic of the word of God.' The absence of the article before καπηλεύοντες seems sufficiently to indicate, that ἐσμεν and καπηλεύοντες are to be taken in immediate connexion; and the only difference in sense between this form and the simpler one of καπηλεύομεν seems to be, that it expresses a habit or continued action rather than a single act. Compare Matthew xxiv. 38 (where by removing the comma usually placed after κατακλυσμοῦ the sense comes out clear as in our authorised version), Mark i. 13 (where ἦν—πειραζόμενος is again improperly separated by a comma), 22, 39; iv. 38; v. 5. Luke i. 21, 22; ii. 33, (a remarkable instance,) iv. 31, 44; xxiv. 53. Acts xiv. 7; xvi. 12; xxii. 19, and other places. But the remark is especially applicable to chap. v. 19 of this Epistle, Θεὸς ἦν ἐν Χριστῷ κόσμον καταλλάσσων ἑαυτῷ*, in which passage

---

* A careful reader will observe the difference between the language of this and the preceding verse. In the former it is, τοῦ καταλ-λάξαντος ἡμᾶς ἑαυτῷ, *who* hath reconciled *us to himself,* because it is spoken of those who were in the Christian church, and therefore

two things appear to me very wonderful: first, that our authorised version among others places a comma at 'Christ'; and second, that the omission of that comma, and the adoption of the construction I am contending for, have been made in former days (and not very remote neither) a ground for a charge of Socinian tendencies. Compare Ephes. iv. 32.

To return to καπηλεύοντες. The passage is rendered by Beza literally, and I conceive accurately, *Non enim, ut plerique, cauponamur sermonem Dei.* The use of καπηλεύω in Æschylus, Theb. 540, is well known: ἔοικεν οὐ καπηλεύσειν μάχην· where Bp. Blomfield in his Glossary writes: "καπηλεύειν *proprie est, to retail.* Anglice verterim hunc locum, *He will fight by wholesale;* quem sensum minus perceperunt interpretes, qui intelligunt καπηλεύειν in secundario sensu, *ob quæstum facere aliquid,* ut in Ennii versu, *Non cauponantes bellum, sed belligerantes.*" Schleusner, to whom the learned Prelate subsequently refers, translates in his Lexicon, *Nos non quæstus et lucri causa tradimus religionem Christianam, eamque corrumpimus.* Just so Parkhurst: *To make a gain of any thing,* especially *by adulterating it with heterogeneous mixtures.* So again Doddridge: "καπηλεύοντες...alludes to the practice of those

---

were supposed to have entered into the reconciliation; and so the Apostle writes to the Colossians, i. 21, καὶ ὑμᾶς ποτὲ ὄντας...νυνὶ δὲ ἀποκατήλλαξεν· whereas in this verse, speaking of the same thing in reference to the *world,* he says, ἦν κόσμον καταλλάσσων— not, *he hath reconciled,* but, *he was reconciling,* went about to reconcile, made a provision for reconciling.

who deal in liquors, which they debase, &c." But why not also, *who deal in liquors* without debasing them? The new idea, of corrupting or debasing, which is consequential from the former and more remote, might doubtless be admitted, if necessary to explain the Apostle's meaning; but most certainly it does not legitimately enter into the translation of the word, nor, as I conceive, even into its interpretation: to me it appears to obscure the sense. It is a pity that Schleusner did not stop at *Christianam.*

. In the contemplation of the awful magnitude of his office, as being to some *a savour of life unto life,* and to others *a savour of death unto death,* the Apostle exclaims, *And who* is *sufficient for these things?* πρὸς ταῦτα τίς ἰκανός; *For* the ministry is not with me a mere work of worldly traffic, but a matter of serious concern: I cannot therefore be content with merely discharging my commission without regard to the results in which it may issue; but take it in hand with a solemn remembrance of the account I must give of it *in the sight of God,* and with a trembling apprehension of its eternal consequences to others. (The passage above quoted from Ennius is, *not making a trade of war, but fighting in earnest.*)

It is implied, that if he dealt with it as a matter of traffic, a mere trade, he need have no fear about his own sufficiency for it: and this is intelligible. On the other hand, if he corrupted and adulterated the word of God, how could this be supposed to make him *sufficient for* his work, or to avert the consequences of it?

The passage generally compared with this, chap. iv. 2,

δολοῦντες τὸν λόγον τοῦ Θεοῦ (cf. 1 Pet. ii. 2, τὸ λογικὸν
ἄδολον γάλα, and Isai. i. 22 (LXX.), οἱ κάπηλοί σου μίσγουσι
τὸν οἶνον ὕδατι), expresses the idea which is not necessarily
included in καπηλεύω, and which therefore ought not to be
foisted in without occasion, much less to the detriment of
the sense*.

iii. 6. *Who also hath made us able ministers.* ὃς καὶ
ἱκάνωσεν ἡμᾶς διακόνους. 'Who also hath fitted us *to be*
ministers.'

Ib. 7. *The ministration of death, written* and *engraven
in stones.* ἡ διακονία τοῦ θανάτου ἐν γράμμασιν, ἐντετυπωμένη
ἐν λίθοις. 'The ministration of death by the letter, engraven in stones.'

Ib. 17. *Now the Lord is that Spirit.* ὁ δὲ Κύριος τὸ
πνεῦμά ἐστιν. 'Now the Lord is the Spirit.' I am utterly
at a loss to imagine what sense our Translators meant to
attach to the passage, in adopting the strange and inaccurate rendering, *that Spirit.* Preserving the plain
literal translation, the sense obviously is, *The Lord* whom
I speak of (see v. 16) *is the Spirit;* or, as it is excellently
paraphrased by Professor Dobree, *Quum loquor de Judæis
AD DOMINUM convertendis, intelligo, A LITERA AD SPIRITUM.*
It is objected, that the Apostle would hardly have mentioned the person of the Holy Spirit as opposed to the
letter of the Mosaic law; but do we not turn to the Holy

---

* I have since found that the same view is taken by Barrow,
(*Pope's Supremacy*, Vol. VI. p. 231. Oxf. 1818.) "That which is
called καπηλεύειν τὸν λόγον τοῦ Θεοῦ, *to make a trade of religion,* will be the great work of the teachers of the church," &c.

Spirit, when we are brought under the influence of his teaching, and enabled by it to receive the spiritual power of the doctrine instead of the dead and killing letter? What our Lord says in John vi. 63, is not unlike this: τὸ πνεῦμά ἐστι τὸ ζωοποιοῦν, ἡ σὰρξ οὐκ ὠφελεῖ οὐδέν.

The common method of interpreting the passage, viz. that the Lord Jesus is the animating Spirit of the Old Testament, appears to me not only to be a mere slurring over of the sense, but to be liable to the fatal objection, that "the Spirit" in the former clause of the verse must be the same with "the Spirit of the Lord" in the latter, in which there is no ambiguity.

Ib. 18. *But we all with open face beholding as in a glass the glory of the Lord.* ἡμεῖς δὲ πάντες ἀνακεκαλυμμένῳ προσώπῳ τὴν δόξαν Κυρίου κατοπτριζόμενοι. 'And we all with unveiled face reflecting as a glass the glory of the Lord.' This differs from Macknight's rendering only in the substitution of *and* for *for*, and 'a glass' for 'mirrors,' the latter of which I adopt as more simple. If the other expression however be preferred as more strictly accurate, it should still be, I think, 'as a mirror,' in the singular.—Let us now look to the sense. Moses, (Exod. xxxiv. 30, 33,) when he came down from the mount, reflected in the shining skin of his face 'the glory of the Lord,' with whom he had been communing, so brightly, that the children of Israel could not look upon him ; and therefore he put a veil upon his face. But we, says the Apostle, v. 13, are "not as Moses, which put a veil over his face:" that veil was an emblem of the obscurity of his dispensation; but we, having such a hope, "use great plainness of speech." And then, after some important and instructive remarks on the subject of this veil in reference to the Jews, he concludes, "We all," meaning *perhaps* all Christians and not ministers only, "reflect the glory of the Lord with our face unveiled;" intimating that the "veil is done away in Christ," and there is no remaining obscurity to be shadowed forth by it.

Ib. ib. Even *as by the Spirit of the Lord.* καθάπερ ἀπὸ Κυρίου πνεύματος. '*Even* as by the Lord, the Spirit.' The marginal translation is, 'Of the Lord, the Spirit'*—where *of* seems to be either a mistake for *by*, or used nearly in the same sense. The translation now proposed is not without difficulty; but neither is any other. It would seem to require ἀπὸ Κυρίου τοῦ πνεύματος, "in like manner as the Article is always inserted in Κύριος ὁ Θεός." (Middleton.) But on the other hand, 'the Spirit of the Lord' in the New Testament is uniformly πνεῦμα (or τὸ πνεῦμα) Κυρίου, and this order we should especially expect to be retained in a passage like the present, where an inversion would involve so serious an ambiguity.

I am determined in favour of the proposed translation by the sense of the passage. Understanding the preceding verse as above explained, the present falls in with that view by referring the effects here stated to the same divine agent, "the Lord the Spirit."

---

* Bishop Middleton in loc. says that the reading of the margin is, *by the Lord of the Spirit.* This, I suppose, is a mere misprint for the marginal reading given above.

iv. 8. We are *troubled*, we are *perplexed*. Θλιβόμενοι, ἀπορούμενοι. 'Being troubled, perplexed.' The participles are closely connected with ἔχομεν in v. 7, and the different clauses furnish so many illustrations of the sentiment expressed in " earthen vessels."

Ib. 13. *We having.* ἔχοντες δέ. 'But having.' · The *we* is unnecessary, as it is repeated at the close of the verse, *we also believe;* and the *but* is absolutely necessary as the link which connects this verse in sense with the preceding. *But*—notwithstanding our afflictions,—yet having the Psalmist's faith, like him *we speak.*

Ib. 15. *That the abundant grace might through the thanksgiving of many redound to the glory of God.* ἵνα ἡ χάρις πλεονάσασα διὰ τῶν πλειόνων τὴν εὐχαριστίαν περισσεύσῃ εἰς τὴν δόξαν τοῦ Θεοῦ. 'That grace abounding by means of many may cause the thanksgiving to abound to the glory of God.'—In the received translation ἡ χάρις πλεονάσασα cannot be *the abundant grace,* neither can διὰ τὴν εὐχαριστίαν be *through the thanksgiving,* which would require τῆς —ίας: neither would the order, τῶν πλειόνων τὴν εὐχαριστίαν, be according to the usage of the Greek Testament. But περισσεύω is both transitive and intransitive, to *abound* and to *make to abound:* see chap. ix. 8 of this Epistle, and 1 Thess. iii. 12. Overlooking this transitive sense, the Vulgate Translator (followed of course by the Rhemish) renders *in gratiarum actione abundet:* whether he found a different reading in his copy of the original, as Beza supposes, seems very doubtful.

v. 1. *If our earthly house of* this *tabernacle were dis-*

6

solved. ἐὰν ἡ ἐπίγειος ἡμῶν οἰκία τοῦ σκήνους καταλυθῇ.
"If the earthly house of our tabernacle be dissolved.'

Ib. 3. *If so be that being clothed.* εἴγε καὶ ἐνδυσάμενοι.
'Since being clothed *with it.*' Literally, ' having put *it* on.'

Ib. 6. *Whilst we are at home in the body.* ἐνδημοῦντες ἐν τῷ σώματι. 'Whilst we are present in the body.' I am sensible that my alteration here is far from being an improvement in this particular clause: the phrase *being at home* expresses the original word much better than that I have substituted for it; and I do not object to it, as some do, on the ground of its implying a *permanent* habitation, for an inn or a lodging is our home while we occupy it. But a translator must look at the whole passage, v. 6—9, and I do not perceive that the beautiful antithesis of ἐκδημεῖν and ἐνδημεῖν can be conveniently preserved by adhering to the expression, *to be at home:* and it is evidently desirable to retain the same idea all through. A middle course, however, might be adopted, viz. to retain the present translation of ἐνδημεῖν in v. 6, and adopt it also in v. 8, *to be at home with the Lord,* (and so far uniformity would be attained in regard to the word ἐνδημεῖν, though still the other rendering must be admitted in v. 9, *present,*) but to express the sense of ἐκδημεῖν as it now is, *be absent.*

Ib. 14. *Then were all dead.* ἄρα οἱ πάντες ἀπέθανον. 'Then all died.' Our Translators by their rendering of the last word intended of course to refer to that spiritual death, out of which the death of Christ was designed to

deliver us. And doubtless the consideration of the great-
ness of the ruin out of which we are delivered furnishes
a powerful argument for our living under the constraining
influences of the love of Christ. But there are strong
objections to this view of the passage: (1) It involves
a strange confusion of terms. The same Greek word ἀπέθανον has two very different senses in the English: *one
died* naturally; *all were dead* spiritually. There is no
parallel between the two; for those who *were* already *dead*,
could not die in the same sense in which they were dead.
(2) When the Apostle does speak of persons as having
been in this state of spiritual death, he expresses it by a
periphrasis, such as νεκρὸς ὢν, Ephes. ii. 1. Coloss. ii. 13.
(3) And above all, ἀπέθανον cannot by any possibility
signify *was dead*. ἀποθνήσκω, *I die;* ἀπέθανον, *I did die* or
AM dead, as in Coloss. iii. 3. *Ye are dead.* A person who
has passed through the act of dying *is* dead.—The use
of ἀπέθανεν in Luke viii. 53, *she was dead*, does not at all
militate against this, as the *proper* translation of the word
there would be *is dead*, but the difference of idiom between the Greek and English languages requires the
change of tense, as in John xi. 13, ἔδοξαν ὅτι—λέγει.
Compare also ver 14 of that chapter. I conclude, then,
that the old translation is untenable.

To the new translation, as a *translation*, no objection
can possibly be made: the difficulty in the way of its
adoption will be the sense it brings out of the passage.
The argument, then, which it presents is this: All believers died with Christ, and are made conformable to his

death and spiritually partakers of it: (Galat. ii. 20.) but as having died with him, they also rose with him: (Romans vi. 5.) and thus living a spiritual life by virtue of his death and resurrection, they do not live to themselves, but to Christ. In this way "the love of Christ constrains" them.—The whole subject is more fully opened in Romans vi. 1—11.

vi. 8. *By honour and dishonour, by evil report and good report.* διὰ δόξης καὶ ἀτιμίας, διὰ δυσφημίας καὶ εὐφημίας. 'Through honour and dishonour, through evil report and good report.' In the preceding verses, 4—7, the original has the same preposition, ἐν, which is first rendered *in,* then *by:* this change may be approved, or at all events allowed; but when the preposition is changed in the original to διὰ, the translation must be varied according to the requirement of the sense.

Ib. 15. *With an infidel.* μετὰ ἀπίστου. 'With an unbeliever'—as the word is rendered in the preceding verse. This was of course the sense in which the word *infidel* was then used: and so in the Collect for Good Friday, 'Jews, Turks (Mahomedans), *infidels* (heathen), and heretics.'

Ib. 17. *And touch not the unclean thing.* καὶ ἀκαθάρτου μὴ ἅπτεσθε. 'And touch no unclean *thing.*' This correction brings the passage into harmony not only with the Greek of which it is a translation, but with the passage of Isaiah (lii. 11) from which it is quoted, and the Hebrew original there.

vii. 8. *With a letter.* ἐν τῇ ἐπιστολῇ. 'By my letter'— viz. the 1st Epistle to the Corinthians.

Ibid. *The same epistle.* ἡ ἐπιστολὴ ἐκείνη. 'That letter.' Why should it be *letter* at the beginning of the verse, and *epistle* at the end?

Ib. 11. *For behold this self-same thing, that ye sorrowed* ... ἰδοὺ γὰρ, αὐτὸ τοῦτο τὸ λυπηθῆναι ὑμᾶς. 'For behold, this very circumstance of your having sorrowed'—

Ibid. *In this matter.* ἐν τῷ πράγματι. 'In the matter.' See on Matthew xv. 12.

viii. 1. *We do you to wit of.* γνωρίζομεν ὑμῖν. 'We certify you of,' or, 'We declare unto you.' The same word as in 1 Corinth. xv. 1.

Ib. 8. *But by occasion of the forwardness of others, and to prove the sincerity of your love.* ἀλλὰ διὰ τῆς ἑτέρων σπουδῆς καὶ τὸ τῆς ὑμετέρας ἀγάπης γνήσιον δοκιμάζων. 'But by the forwardness of others to prove the sincerity of your love also.' It is clear that διὰ τῆς σπουδῆς is dependent on δοκιμάζων, and the force of καὶ is to mark more strongly the opposition between ἑτέρων and ὑμετέρας —of yours as well as theirs.

ix. 5. *Whereof ye had notice before.* τὴν προκατηγγελμένην. 'Whereof notice had been given before'—i. e. I think, given *by* the Corinthians, not *to* them. They had announced their readiness to make the contribution. It is, however, perhaps doubtful.

x. 6. *And having in a readiness.* καὶ ἐν ἑτοίμῳ ἔχοντες. 'And being ready.' The common translation is strange indeed. The expression of the original is, it must be confessed, an uncommon form; but it is evidently equivalent to ἑτοίμως ἔχοντες, which again is equivalent to ἕτοιμοι ὄντες, as our Translators have rightly understood it in Acts xxi. 13, and in chap. xii. 14 of this Epistle.—The verb ἔχω in the sense of *sum* is generally connected with an adverb, to which it is clear that the adjective with a preposition nearly approximates. Compare 1 Pet. iv. 5, τῷ ἑτοίμως ἔχοντι. Instances however are not wanting, in which it is found joined with a preposition and substantive: Eurip. Suppl. 164, ἐν μὲν αἰσχύναις ἔχω, with which Dobree compares Bacch. 89, ἔχουσ' ἐν . . . ἀνάγκαισι.

Ib. 9. *That I may not seem.* ἵνα δὲ μὴ δόξω 'But, that I may not seem'—Griesbach indeed omits the δὲ, which to me appears necessary to the sense; especially if we arrange the passage, as I think it clearly ought to be arranged with Griesbach, viz. putting a colon, or rather a comma, at the end of v. 9, and then including v. 10 in a parenthesis, that the connexion may be: *But, that I may not seem as if I would terrify you by letters,* [*my letters,* it should be,] (*For his letters, say they,* &c.) *Let such an one,* &c.—The common translation and arrangement makes an awkward connexion between the 9th verse and the 8th.

Ib. 10. *Say they.* φησι. 'Saith one.' There is an evident reference to the singular number in the ὁ τοιοῦτος of the next verse.

xi. 16. *That I may boast myself a little.* ἵνα μικρόν τι κἀγὼ καυχήσωμαι. 'That I also may boast myself a little.' I, as well as they. See ver. 18.

xii. 2, 3. *I knew.* οἶδα. 'I know of,' or 'I know.' Not only has οἶδα never a past sense; but it was beside the

Apostle's purpose to mention his having formerly known such a person: he rather refers to his present knowledge of him, intimating that he could mention him, if he deemed it expedient to disclose the whole.

Ibid. *Above fourteen years ago.* πρὸ ἐτῶν δεκατεσσάρων. 'Fourteen years ago.' In some few editions *above* has got changed to *about*. But the literal translation is, *before fourteen years,* i. e. *fourteen years before this time,* or *ago.*

Ib. 4. *It is not lawful.* οὐκ ἐξόν. 'It is not possible,' as in the margin.

Ib. 18. *A brother.* τὸν ἀδελφόν. 'The brother.' See chap. viii. 18, 22.

xiii. 3. *Of Christ speaking in me, which to you-ward is not weak.* τοῦ ἐν ἐμοὶ λαλοῦντος Χριστοῦ, ὃς εἰς ὑμᾶς οὐκ ἀσθενεῖ. 'Of Christ speaking by me, who is not weak towards you.' The *which* is ambiguous; and the words *towards you* are better placed after *is not weak,* that they may be less emphatic, the opposition of the two clauses lying in ἀσθενεῖ and δυνατεῖ.

THE EPISTLE TO THE GALATIANS.

Chap. i. 4. *That he might deliver us from this present evil world.* ὅπως ἐξέληται ἡμᾶς ἐκ τοῦ ἐνεστῶτος αἰῶνος πονηροῦ. 'That ho might deliver us from out of the present evil world'—or, 'from among.' See on Acts ii. 40.

Ib. 6. *Unto another gospel.* εἰς ἕτερον εὐαγγέλιον. 'Unto a strange gospel.' As it follows immediately, ὃ οὐκ ἔστιν ἄλλο, it is clearly desirable to distinguish between ἕτερον and ἄλλο in the translation. Ἑτέρας is rendered *strange* in Jude, 7. Some understand οὐκ ἔστιν ἄλλο as if it were equivalent to οὐδὲν ἄλλο, *which is no other* thing *than*—But εἰ μὴ is used here in the same sense as ἐὰν μὴ in chap. ii. 17, for which see on Luke iv. 26, 27.—For ἕτερον, ἄλλο εὐαγγελίον compare 2 Corinth. xi. 4.

Ib. 10. *For do I now persuade men, or God? or do I seek to please men?* ἄρτι γὰρ ἀνθρώπους πείθω, ἢ τὸν Θεόν; ἢ ζητῶ ἀνθρώποις ἀρέσκειν; 'For am I now seeking the favour of men, or of God? or am I aiming to please men?' The word πείθω seems to be here used in the same sense as in Acts xii. 20, *having persuaded Blastus, having made him their friend*, as pointed out by Dr. Doddridge, though his other examples are, I think, less to the purpose. The change I have made in the translation removes the obscurity and ambiguity of the passage.

ii. 2. *And communicated unto them that Gospel which I preach among the Gentiles, but privately to them which were of reputation.* καὶ ἀνεθέμην αὐτοῖς τὸ εὐαγγέλιον ὃ κηρύσσω ἐν τοῖς ἔθνεσι, κατ' ἰδίαν δὲ τοῖς δοκοῦσι. 'And communicated unto them the gospel which I preach among the Gentiles, but privately to those who were high in reputation'—i. e. publicly to the whole church, and privately, in a private conference, to the leading Apostles.— The alterations here proposed are unimportant in themselves; but they are in a measure necessary to clear the way for what follows, "in which are some things hard to be understood" in the original, but in our common translation, I think, unintelligible.—Upon the present verse, then, we are to observe, that two important words, ἀνεθέμην and τοῖς δοκοῦσι, will occur again, and it is desirable to settle them in some way of rendering which may be conveniently preserved throughout. The former has occurred already in chap. i. 16. The latter occurs twice in v. 6, and once in v. 9, with some variation; but in vv. 2 and 6, οἱ δοκοῦντες used absolutely bears the same sense as οἱ δοκοῦντες εἶναί τι, and the phrase is so used in classical writers, ex. gr. Eurip. Hec. 295. In all the three verses we are clearly to understand it of Peter, James, and John, who are specified in v. 9.—From the concluding words of v. 2 it is evident that St Paul's object in his conference with the other Apostles was to satisfy his own mind, and especially theirs, that the gospel which he preached was the true gospel of Jesus Christ; because otherwise he would have *run in vain.*

Ib. 3—4. *But neither Titus, who was with me, being a Greek, was compelled to be circumcised: And that because of false brethren unawares brought in, who came in privily to spy out our liberty.* ἀλλ' οὐδὲ Τίτος ὁ σὺν ἐμοὶ, Ἕλλην ὢν, ἠναγκάσθη περιτμηθῆναι· διὰ δὲ τοὺς παρεισάκτους ψευδαδέλφους, οἵτινες παρεισῆλθον κατασκοπῆσαι τὴν ἐλευθερίαν ἡμῶν. 'But neither Titus, who was with me, being a Greek, was under any necessity to be circumcised, But only because of the false brethren who were insidiously brought in, who came in privily to spy out our liberty:'

i. e. there was no necessity for his being circumcised, except that pretended necessity which was set up by these false brethren. See Acts xvi. 3. I have inserted *only* to make the sense clearer; but perhaps *except* might be substituted for *but*, and *only* omitted.

Now, with respect to the authorised translation, I profess not to understand it. Griesbach seems inclined to alter the text, and connect the beginning of v. 4 with v. 5, as if it were τοῖς ψευδαδέλφοις. Doddridge and Dobree agree in understanding v. 4 as assigning a reason why Paul would not have Titus circumcised: "ne Judaïzantibus istis morem gererem." In my view his opposition to these false teachers does not commence till v. 5, and in v. 4 he states the only shadow of reason there was for it, which he afterwards says he would not yield to. *Unawares brought in* can hardly be admitted as the correct translation.

Ib. 6. *But of those who seemed to be somewhat, whatsoever they were, it maketh no matter to me: God accepteth no man's person: for they who seemed to be somewhat in conference added nothing to me.*—I subjoin the original with what I conceive to be the proper marks of punctuation: ἀπὸ δὲ τῶν δοκούντων εἶναί τι, (ὁποῖοί ποτε ἦσαν, οὐδέν μοι διαφέρει· πρόσωπον Θεὸς ἀνθρώπου οὐ λαμβάνει,) ἐμοὶ γὰρ οἱ δοκοῦντες οὐδὲν προσανέθεντο. 'But of those who were high in reputation, (whatsoever they were, it maketh no matter to me; God accepteth no man's person,) those, I say, who were high in reputation communicated nothing new to me.'

Of those who were high in reputation.] I have deviated from the common translation for the reason stated on v. 2, but I have retained the same form with regard to ἀπὸ, which might have been rendered more correctly, *on the part of those.*—But two things seem to me clear; first, that it is itself an irregular sentence, the writer having begun with one form, and concluded with another: we should have expected, *on the part of &c. nothing new was communicated to me.* Next, that the insertion of the parenthesis was the occasion of this variation, and that then οἱ δοκοῦντες is the repetition of ἀπὸ τῶν δοκούντων in accordance with the altered form of the sentence. Such an anomalous construction is quite in St Paul's manner, and is entirely consistent with the practice of classical writers.

Whatsoever they were, &c.] The object of this parenthesis, which makes such strange confusion with the common punctuation, is to preclude the idea of his having bowed to the authority even of the chief of the Apostles. He had received his gospel from God independently of them (chap. i. 12); and when he compared it with theirs, the identity resulting was a striking evidence of its truth and divine origin.

Those, I say] When in a sentence of this irregular form the leading idea is repeated after an interruption of the regular train of thought, δὲ or γὰρ is generally inserted in classical writers with the repeated words. In such a case γὰρ has nearly the force of *verily* (see on Rom. v. 7): I have here expressed it by *I say.*

Communicated nothing new to me] Common translation,

in conference added nothing to me. If it had been, *added nothing to my gospel*, it would have been at least intelligible, which, I apprehend, in its present form it is not. Now, in v. 2, ἀνεθέμην is properly rendered *communicated*; and therefore προσανέθεντο here is, *communicated in addition*. (In chap. i. 16, unless the πρὸς in προσανεθέμην be redundant, it must signify, that having received his commission from God he did not, *in addition to that*, communicate with flesh and blood.) In the present passage we gain great advantage by preserving uniformity, because it keeps up the connexion with the ἀνεθέμην of v. 2. He communicated his gospel to them, that they might be satisfied of its being the true and full gospel; and if there had been any thing wrong or defective in it, they would have communicated to him whatever was necessary to correct or supply it. But they *communicated nothing new:* they set to it the seal of their testimony, that it was the gospel which they themselves preached.

Ib. 7—9. It is evident in these verses that ἰδόντες and γνόντες are connected together, and that both are in concord with Ἰάκωβος καὶ Κηφᾶς καὶ Ἰωάννης. But by interposing the nominatives *between the two* participles, whereas in the original they come, correctly enough, after both, our Translators have broken off this connexion, and introduced confusion. I would correct and arrange as follows:

'But contrariwise, when James and Cephas and John, who were reputed to be pillars, saw that the gospel of the uncircumcision was committed unto me, as *that* of the cir-

cumcision was to Peter; (For he that wrought ——
toward the Gentiles ;) And when they perceived the grace
that was given unto me, they gave, &c.'

Ib. 17. Is *therefore Christ the minister of sin?* ἄρα
Χριστὸς ἁμαρτίας διάκονος; ' *Is* not then Christ a minister
of sin?' I am not aware of any other example of ἄρα
used in this sense in the New Testament. (For examples
in the poets see Bp. Monk's note on Eurip. Alcest. 351.)
But in so rendering it here I am countenanced by the high
authority of Tyndale; and it seems to be required by
the sense of the passage. 'If we are found sinners, found
guilty and condemned, while seeking to be justified by
Christ (rather, *in Christ*) ; does it not follow as a necessary
conclusion from this, that Christ is *a minister of sin*, and
his gospel, like the law (2 Corinth. iii. 7, 9), a *ministration
of condemnation and death?*' Such a conclusion is to be
rejected as most dishonourable to Christ; and Peter's
conduct was reprehensible in this, that it gave countenance to the premises from which such a conclusion must
follow. Our translation assumes the correctness of the
premises, and denies the conclusion drawn from them.
The amended translation denies the premises on account
of the objectionable conclusion to which they would
lead.

Ib. 20. *Nevertheless I live, yet not I.* ζῶ δὲ οὐκέτι ἐγώ.
'And I no longer live.' The difference between these two
translations is considerable, and I do not deny that there
is something to be said in favour of the old one, because it
may seem, that admitting the new way, the Apostle would

not have separated the οὐκ and the δέ. I cannot however
think that his intention was to make the broad statement,
nevertheless I live, and then to modify it, as our translation
does.

iii. 17. *The covenant that was confirmed before of God
in Christ.* διαθήκην προκεκυρωμένην ὑπὸ τοῦ Θεοῦ εἰς Χρι-
στόν. 'A covenant before confirmed of God with Christ'
—or even, 'to Christ.' The words εἰς Χριστὸν are wanting
in some MSS. and therefore in some versions; but I believe our own version is the earliest which renders them
'in Christ.' This rendering might doubtless be admitted,
if necessary to the clear expression of the sentiment; but
here it seems only to obscure it, when taken in connexion
with the following verses.—Both Tyndale and Cranmer
translate, 'unto Christ-ward.' Compare for the expression
2 Cor. ii. 8, κυρῶσαι εἰς αὐτὸν ἀγάπην, and in confirmation
of the sentiment v. 19 of the present chapter, where ᾧ
ἐπήγγελται, *to whom the promise was made,* (which I cannot
but consider the right translation,) is in substance equivalent to, *with whom the covenant was made.* Compare also
for different constructions after διαθήκη Hebr. viii. 8, 9,
διαθήκην ἐπὶ τὸν οἶκον, and τοῖς πατράσιν αὐτῶν· and ix. 20,
πρὸς ὑμας.

That the covenant of the gospel, in its original and
proper sense, is a covenant made not between God and
man, but between God and Christ, seems to be laid down
as the basis of the argument. The law, which came in
afterwards, was ordained or arranged by the intervention
or instrumentality of angels through a mediator. 'But

a mediator is not of one,'—has relation not to one party, but to more than one; implying therefore the possibility of the covenant being broken by the one or the other: 'but God is one;' and in the gospel-covenant though the contracting parties, God and Christ, are two persons, they are one in Godhead: and therefore there is no possibility of a breach of covenant; and therefore no mediator and no witness is required.

Into this covenant, thus made with Christ, man enters by faith in Christ. When by faith he is in Christ, he is in the covenant, and entitled to its benefits on the ground of Christ's having fulfilled the conditions. Bishop Hopkins calls it "the covenant of redemption" as between God and Christ, and "the covenant of reconciliation" as between God and man. See his *Doctrine of the Two Covenants* in the 2nd volume of his works, Pratt's edition.

Ibid. *Cannot disannul.* οὐκ ἀκυροῖ. 'Does not disannul'—ἀκυροῖ being the *indicative* present, though its contracted form presents the appearance of an optative.

Ib. 22. *That the promise by faith of Jesus Christ might be given to them that believe.* ἵνα ἡ ἐπαγγελία ἐκ πίστεως Ἰησοῦ Χριστοῦ δοθῇ τοῖς πιστεύουσι. 'That the promise may be given to believers through faith in Jesus Christ.' The common order connects ἐκ πίστεως, &c. with ἡ ἐπαγγελία, as if it were ἡ ἐκ πίστεως. The words *through faith in Jesus Christ* appear to me to mark the *way* in which the fulfilment of the promise is to be obtained.

iv. 4. *Made of a woman, made under the law.* γενόμενον ἐκ γυναικὸς, γενόμενον ὑπὸ νόμον. 'Born of a woman, born under the law,' or rather perhaps, 'made subject to the law.' It seems to have been by some confusion in reference to this common sense of γενέσθαι ὑπό τινα, that our Translators were led (for uniformity's sake?) to the strange expression, *made of a woman.* So in Romans i. 3, *which was made* (born) *of the seed of David according to the flesh.*

Ib. 17. *They zealously affect you,* (marg. *us,*] but *not well; yea, they would exclude you, that ye might affect them.* ζηλοῦσιν ὑμᾶς οὐ καλῶς, ἀλλὰ ἐκκλεῖσαι ὑμᾶς (text. rec. ἡμᾶς) θέλουσιν, ἵνα αὐτοὺς ζηλοῦτε. 'They do not well affect you, but desire to exclude us, that ye may affect them.' Griesbach's reading after most MSS. is ὑμᾶς, but the sense so obviously requires ἡμᾶς, that a smaller amount of authority will justify its restoration.—In the common translation the adverb *zealously* is prefixed to *affect,* to give (I suppose) a complete expression to the sense of ζηλοῦσιν. But it does not add to the clearness of the idea; and it introduces an awkwardness far removed from the simplicity of the original by making an opposition between affecting *zealously* and affecting *well.*

Ib. 20. *I desire.* ἤθελον δέ. 'I could wish'—like ηὐχόμην in Romans ix. 3. In strictness it ought to be, 'I could wish however;' but perhaps upon the whole it may be considered better to pass over δέ as redundant.

v. 12. *Which trouble you.* οἱ ἀναστατοῦντες ὑμᾶς. 'Who unsettle you.' Not the same word which is translated *trouble* in v. 10.

vi. 11. *Ye see how large a letter I have written unto you
with mine own hand.* ἴδετε πηλίκοις ὑμῖν γράμμασιν ἔγραψα
τῇ ἐμῇ χειρί. 'See in what large letters I write to you
with mine own hand.'—"How large a letter I have written
to you," is the translation of Tyndale's, Cranmer's, and
the Geneva bibles, besides our own; and thus they understand it of the whole epistle as written by Paul himself.
Wicliffe has, "Se ye what maner lettris I have write,"
which is perhaps ambiguous: the Rhemish version somewhat better, "See with what manner of letters I have
written:" Doddridge, "Ye see with what large letters I
have written *this epistle*"—rightly arguing, after Whitby,
that "St. Paul never uses the word γράμματα when he
speaks of his epistles."

But it does not seem to have been observed, that the
more idiomatic rendering of ἔγραψα is, *I write;* and that
it refers with quite as much propriety to what he is just
beginning to write as to what he had written already. I
consider therefore these concluding verses as a postscript
to the letter, written by the Apostle's own hand after the
letter itself had been penned by his amanuensis. In it he
hastily touches off a few pregnant hints, embodying in a
brief summary not the argument that was to persuade
their judgment, but the deep and powerful feelings that
were to stir their inmost hearts. (See 1 Cor. xvi. 21—4,
as an illustration of the same thing.) Of such a concluding appeal, written by his own hand, and shutting up all
discussion in the grand principles of the truth of the
gospel, the effect upon the honest minds and Christian

hearts in the Galatian church may be conceived by the impression which even now it makes upon our own.

Ib. *By whom.* δι' οὗ. 'By which,' or, as in the margin, 'whereby.' It is much more simple to make σταυρῷ the antecedent, than Χριστοῦ.

THE EPISTLE TO THE EPHESIANS.

CHAP. i. 1. *To the saints which are at Ephesus, and to the faithful in Christ Jesus.* τοῖς ἁγίοις τοῖς οὖσιν ἐν Ἐφέσῳ καὶ πιστοῖς ἐν Χριστῷ Ἰησοῦ. 'To the saints and faithful in Christ Jesus, which are in Ephesus.'

Ib. 3. *The God and Father of our Lord Jesus Christ.* ὁ Θεὸς καὶ πατὴρ τοῦ Κυρίου ἡμῶν Ἰησοῦ Χριστοῦ. 'God the Father of our Lord Jesus Christ.' See the note on 1 Corinth. xv. 24.

Ib. 13. *In whom ye also* trusted, *after that ye heard the word of truth, the gospel of your salvation; in whom also after that ye believed, ye were sealed with that holy Spirit of promise.* ἐν ᾧ καὶ ὑμεῖς, ἀκούσαντες τὸν λόγον τῆς ἀληθείας, τὸ εὐαγγέλιον τῆς σωτηρίας ὑμῶν, ἐν ᾧ καὶ πιστεύσαντες, ἐσφραγίσθητε τῷ πνεύματι τῆς ἐπαγγελίας τῷ ἁγίῳ. 'In whom ye also, having heard the word of truth, the gospel of your salvation, and believed on him, were sealed with the holy Spirit of promise.' There can be no doubt, I think, that our Translators have enervated the sense of the passage by dividing it into two finite sentences. I consider it also clear, that the latter ἐν ᾧ is little more than a repetition of the former; yet so, that while the former refers immediately to ἐσφραγίσθητε (in whom ye were sealed), the latter has a joint reference to both the words, πιστεύσαντες and ἐσφραγίσθητε, with which it stands connected. If this view is correct, it will not be considered too great a liberty to express the latter ἐν ᾧ as I have done, 'Having believed in him*.'

ii. 15—6. *For to make in himself of twain one new man, so making peace; and that he might reconcile*—ἵνα τοὺς δύο κτίσῃ ἐν ἑαυτῷ εἰς ἕνα καινὸν ἄνθρωπον, ποιῶν εἰρήνην· καὶ ἀποκαταλλάξῃ—'That he might made the two one new man in himself, making peace *between them;* And might reconcile'—'the two' being of course Jews and Gentiles. And, the work here largely described consisting of two parts,—making peace between Jews and Gentiles, and then between God and men,—the former is expressed in the 15th verse, and it seems desirable to mark the εἰρήνη intended by the words I have added.—The translation in the authorised version of ἵνα κτίσῃ καὶ ἀποκαταλλάξῃ, *for to make and that he might reconcile,* has an awkwardness in it that must be got rid of.

---

* Another view of the whole of this interesting passage is suggested to me by a Friend, and is entitled to careful consideration. It proposes to make, as our Translators do, two finite sentences of ver. 13, but after ὑμεῖς to supply ἐκληρώθητε instead of ἐπιστεύσατε, so that the connexion of the whole will be as follows:

v. 7. ἐν ᾧ ἔχομεν...

11. ἐν ᾧ καὶ ἐκληρώθημεν...

13. ἐν ᾧ καὶ ὑμεῖς (ἐκληρώθητε)...ἐν ᾧ καὶ πιστεύσαντες ἐσφραγίσθητε...

Ib. 17. *And came and preached.* καὶ ἐλθὼν εὐηγγελί-
σατο. 'And he came and preached.' It is a new sentence
resumed from v. 14, *He is our peace,* and cannot be connected in the same sentence with v. 16.

iii. 2. *If ye have heard.* εἴγε ἠκούσατε. 'Since ye have
heard.' So in chap. iv. 21, *since, for, if so be.* See on
2 Corinth. v. 3.

Ib. 8. *That I should preach.* εὐαγγελίσασθαι. 'To
preach.' The change is proposed only that it may har-
monise with the φωτίσαι following, *to make all* men *see.*

Ib. 10. *By the church.* διὰ τῆς ἐκκλησίας. 'Through
the church:' i. e. *by means of.*

iv. 15. *Speaking the truth.* ἀληθεύοντες. 'Holding
the truth.' Marg. *being sincere.* The common translation
seems to restrict the sense to ministers; the marginal, to
be too general.

Ib. 16. *Compacted by that which every joint supplieth,*
according to the effectual working in the measure of every
part. συμβιβαζόμενον διὰ πάσης ἁφῆς τῆς ἐπιχορηγίας κατ᾽
ἐνέργειαν ἐν μέτρῳ ἑνὸς ἑκάστου μέρους. (I have omitted the
comma usually placed after ἐπιχορηγίας, as being doubtful.)
I must as much despair of satisfying others with any new
translation here, as of satisfying myself with the received version. I will therefore offer first some introductory
remarks.——I used to think that the construction adopted
by our venerable Translators was, διὰ τῆς ἐπιχορηγίας πάσης
ἁφῆς, and that the meaning of their version was, *com-*
pacted by that (matter or nourishment) *which supplieth*
every joint: but perhaps I ought to have understood it,

compacted through every joint of supply, i. e. every joint
being the instrument of sending forward the supply to
the next part or member. To the former sense I conceive
the Greek construction to be opposed, the governing noun
in Regimen having the Article, and the governed not
having it. With regard to the latter, the expression itself,
so understood, is obscure (I find some render the words,
juncturæ subministrationis); and the words of our Translators express this sense very obscurely: they might have
said, 'compacted by *the nourishment* which every joint
supplieth.'

Now, it is suggested by Professor Dobree that ἐπιχο-
ρηγία may be the *materia suppeditata,* ὕλη, which contains
a hint I am inclined to make use of; (compare the use
of the word in Philipp. i. 19.) and I find that Griesbach
places the comma after ἐνέργειαν, which also appears to
me very plausible. Premising this, and comparing the
whole passage, as must necessarily be done, with its parallel, Coloss. ii. 19 (ἐξ οὗ πᾶν τὸ σῶμα διὰ τῶν ἁφῶν καὶ
συνδέσμων ἐπιχορηγούμενον καὶ συμβιβαζόμενον, where the
construction of διὰ τῶν ἁφῶν after the participles makes
a strong argument for taking διὰ πάσης ἁφῆς here in a
similar way,) I would suggest as follows:

'Compacted through every joint, according to the
effectual working of the nourishment supplied, in the
measure of every part.'

Dobree would take ἐν μέτρῳ by itself, *in a certain determinate measure,* and connect κατ' ἐνέργειαν ἑνὸς ἑκάστου
μέρους. But I do not see any objection to connecting ἐν

μέτρῳ ἑνὸς ἑκάστου μέρους, and understanding it, *according to the measure* communicated *to every part.*

Ib. 18. *Through the ignorance that is in them.* διὰ τὴν ἄγνοιαν τὴν οὖσαν ἐν αὐτοῖς. 'Because of the ignorance that is in them,' as the preposition is correctly translated in the next clause. See above on Matthew xv. 3, 6.

Ib. 24. *In righteousness and true holiness.* ἐν δικαιο- σύνῃ καὶ ὁσιότητι τῆς ἀληθείας. 'In the righteousness and holiness of the truth.' If the other form be adopted, it should at least be, *in true righteousness and holiness,* the τῆς ἀληθείας having reference to both the other substantives.

Ib. 32. *God for Christ's sake hath forgiven you.* ὁ Θεὸς ἐν Χριστῷ ἐχαρίσατο ὑμῖν. 'God in Christ hath for- given you.' The sentiment and form of expression are the same as in 2 Cor. v. 19: and the literal rendering in both cases presents it with sufficient clearness, besides having the advantage of simplicity and uniformity.

v. 5. *In the kingdom of Christ and of God.* ἐν τῇ βα- σιλείᾳ τοῦ Χριστοῦ καὶ Θεοῦ. 'Of Christ and God.' The principle upon which this correction is made is now so generally understood, that I need not enlarge upon it. Our Translators have rendered it, as if it were καὶ τοῦ Θεοῦ. If the Article had been repeated before Θεοῦ, it would have indicated that two different persons were in- tended by Χριστοῦ and Θεοῦ. For a full investigation of the whole question the Reader is referred to Bishop Mid- dleton's work.

Ib. 13. *But all things that are reproved, are made manifest by the light.* τὰ δὲ πάντα ἐλεγχόμενα ὑπὸ τοῦ φωτὸς φανεροῦται. 'But all things are reproved and made manifest by the light.' Or, 'But all things when reproved by the light are made manifest.' The common translation would certainly require τὰ before ἐλεγχόμενα. Some editions place a comma at ἐλεγχόμενα, Griesbach at πάντα and φωτὸς, which I think better; but I have admitted neither, conceiving that ὑπὸ τοῦ φωτὸς is connected with both the participle and verb.—In the latter clause of the verse I acquiesce, after some hesitation, in the authorised translation, understanding φανερούμενον as a middle participle in an active sense; and then the sentiment is, that as children of light they should reprove and make manifest the works of darkness, it being the nature of light to do this*.

Ib. 19. *Speaking to yourselves.* λαλοῦντες ἑαυτοῖς. 'Speaking to one another.' Compare Coloss. iii. 16. Also the well-known passage of Pliny, Lib. x. Epist. 97: *Carmen Christo quasi Deo dicere secum* INVICEM.

vi. 12. *Against spiritual wickedness in high places.* πρὸς τὰ πνευματικὰ τῆς πονηρίας ἐν τοῖς ἐπουρανίοις. 'Against the

---

* But upon further consideration this rendering of φανερούμενον appears to me so unnatural after the passive φανεροῦται, and the sense produced by it so insipid and scarcely intelligible, that I venture on another attempt: 'For all that is made manifest is light'— i. e. the darkness of heathen abominations, when exposed and reproved by the holy conversation of Christians, becomes as it were day-light, is penetrated with a light calculated to convince them of their guilt, and so lead them to repentance. And to this the following clause seems to agree : *Awake—and Christ shall give thee light.* Φῶς for φωτεινὸν, nearly as in ver. 8.

spiritual *powers* of wickedness in the air.' The marginal reading is, *against wicked spirits in heavenly places*: Professor Dobree corrects, *the spiritual* agents *of wickedness in the sky* or *air*. If *powers* be received instead of *agents*, as being rather more simple, the ἐξουσίας before might be rendered *dominions*.—For the doctrine compare chap. ii. 2.

Ib. 16. *Of the wicked.* τοῦ πονηροῦ. 'Of the wicked one.' The same words are properly so translated in Matt. xiii. 38.

THE EPISTLE TO THE PHILIPPIANS.

CHAP. i. 7. *Partakers of my grace.* συγκοινωνούς μου τῆς χάριτος. 'Partakers with me of grace,' as in the margin ; and I the rather point this out, because I have heard an opinion expressed, that Θεοῦ συνεργοὶ, 1 Corinth. iii. 9, ought not to be rendered *labourers together with God*, for that that sense would require Θεῷ, and therefore, *a fortiori*, in 2 Corinth. vi. 1, our Translators are wrong in supplying *with him* after συνεργοῦντες. But this criticism is, like many others of the present day, an erroneous refinement: few things are more common in Greek than the Genitive after words so compounded with σύν. Romans viii. 17. Philem. 1. Revelat. xix. 10. Herod. ii. 134. σύνδουλος Αἰσώπου, Soph. Antig. 451. ξύνοικος τῶν κάτω θεῶν, may be taken as a sample ; and any reader of Greek may add to the collection almost without end from any author he may take in hand.

Ib. 10. *That ye may approve things that are excellent.* εἰς τὸ δοκιμάζειν ὑμᾶς τὰ διαφέροντα. 'That ye may try things that differ.' See Romans ii. 18, and the margin in both places.

Ib. 22. *But if I live in the flesh, this* is *the fruit of my labour : yet what I shall choose I wot not.* εἰ δὲ τὸ ζῆν ἐν σαρκὶ τοῦτό μοι καρπὸς ἔργου, καὶ τί αἱρήσομαι, οὐ γνωρίζω. 'But whether this living in the flesh be worth my while, or what I shall choose, I know not.'—Most of those who adopt this mode of translating, consider τοῦτο as merely redundant, perhaps rightly; but it does not seem necessary. The common translation has great difficulties : something must be supplied to complete the sense in the first clause, and something understood to explain the meaning of τοῦτο, and a very unusual sense must be given to καὶ, *yet :* and after all, the line of argument is by no means clear. If *worth my while* be thought too familiar, we may adopt from Beza, *profitable for me.*—The Roman Catholics get over the difficulty very ingeniously, as follows : *And if to live in the flesh, this is to me the fruit of labour : and what I shall choose I know not.*

Ib. 24. *More needful for you.* ἀναγκαιότερον δι' ὑμᾶς. 'More needful for your sakes.'

ii. 3. Let *nothing* be done. μηδέν. '*Doing* nothing.' It is much simpler to insert the participle, and then retain the same form in ἡγούμενοι following.

Ib. 15. *Of a crooked and perverse nation.* γενεᾶς σκολιᾶς καὶ διεστραμμένης. '.Of an untoward and perverse generation.' As the words γενεᾶς σκολιᾶς occur in Acts ii.

40, it is better to preserve uniformity of translation; though of σκολιᾶς perhaps the other rendering, *crooked*, might better be retained in both places.

Ib. 17. *Yea, and if I be offered.* ἀλλ᾽ εἰ καὶ σπένδομαι. 'But even if I be poured out.' The allusion to the drink-offering poured out on the sacrifice offered is too clear to be mistaken; and as the sacrifice is here expressly mentioned, it is necessary to retain the distinguishing idea. In 2 Tim. iv. 6, where the word is similarly used, it is without any mention of the sacrifice, and therefore the general term *offered* is less objectionable.

Ib. 18. *For the same cause.* τὸ δ᾽ αὐτό. 'In like manner.'

Ib. 25. *But your messenger, and he that ministered to my wants.* ὑμῶν δὲ ἀπόστολον καὶ λειτουργὸν τῆς χρείας μου. 'But your messenger and minister to my wants:' i. e. employed by you to minister to my wants. There is no doubt that ὑμῶν belongs to λειτουργὸν equally with ἀπόστολον.

iv. 2. *I beseech Euodias.* Εὐοδίαν παρακαλῶ. 'I beseech Euodia.' The whole tenor of the passage seems to make it plain that it is the name of a woman. See on the next verse.

Ib. 3. *Help those women which laboured.* συλλαμβάνου αὐταῖς, αἵτινες συνήθλησαν. 'Help them, since they laboured.' I understand αὐταῖς here in its strictly relative sense, Εὐοδίαν καὶ Συντύχην being antecedents to it; and he urges the person addressed to render a service of Christian charity to those pious women by assisting to reconcile their differences, enforcing it by a consideration of the services they had rendered him in the gospel.

This is not a forced sense of αἵτινες, which differs from the simple relative ὅς, though it is sometimes used in the same way: compare Acts xvii. 11, οἵτινες ἐδέξαντο τὸν λόγον, *in that they received the word*, as it is well rendered. See also James iv. 14, 1 Corinth. vi. 20. — It may be doubted whether the Greek language would allow of αὐταῖς used in the sense which our Translators give it here, and followed by αἵτινες. In 1 Pet. i. 12 we have αὐτὰ ἅ, but the other form I do not remember to have observed*.

Ib. 8. *If* there be *any virtue, and if* there be *any praise.* εἴ τις ἀρετή, καὶ εἴ τις ἔπαινος. 'Whatever virtue and whatever praise *there be.*' This is the almost universal sense of εἴ τις, which of course does not express any doubt of the existence of the thing in the abstract.

Ib. 15. *Now, ye Philippians, know also.* οἴδατε δὲ καὶ ὑμεῖς, Φιλιππήσιοι. 'And yourselves also know, O Philippians.' The other reading makes οἴδατε an imperative mood. I must however in justice observe, that this gross blunder belongs not to our Translators, but to our printers. In all the early editions of the authorised version which I have inspected, extending from 1612 to 1666, it stands

---

* A seeming exception to this remark, but only seeming, occurs in Eurip. Troad. 662, ἀπέπτυσ' αὐτήν, ἥτις—but there ἥτις is evidently used in its indefinite sense, *whoever: whoever* &c. *her I loathe.* The case before us entirely differs from this, as αὐταῖς manifestly refers to the women already mentioned, and cannot admit the other sense, *whoever.* In Soph. Œd. Col. 263, οἵτινες is equivalent to ἐπεὶ ὑμεῖς.

correctly pointed, *Now ye Philippians know also* : in nearly all the modern editions I have seen, including those printed under the superintendence of private editors, the error is found*. I have varied from the authorised translation only to avoid ambiguity.

Ib. 17. *A gift.* τὸ δόμα. 'The gift'—viz. that which they had sent to him.

THE EPISTLE TO THE COLOSSIANS.

CHAP. i. 19. *For it pleased* the Father *that in him should all fulness dwell.* ὅτι ἐν αὐτῷ εὐδόκησε πᾶν τὸ πλήρωμα κατοικῆσαι. 'For all the fulness *of the Godhead* was pleased to dwell in him.' In the received version, first of all, there is a strange grammatical confusion : *It pleased* the Father *that in him should all fulness dwell, and ... by him to reconcile.* This at all events *must* be corrected. And the next point is even more important. The construction of εὐδόκησε as an impersonal verb followed by a case (τῷ Πατρὶ) is one unknown to the Greek language; and the universal usage in the New Testament is in strict accordance with the general rule. The three forms under

---

* So all the modern editions in Philipp. i. 30, print *and* in the Italic character, though it is found, as far as I know, in all the Greek copies, and is printed accordingly in all the old series of English editions.—Both these errors are likely to be henceforth corrected in the copies printed at the Cambridge Press.

which it occurs are the following : Matth. iii. 17, ἐν ᾧ εὐδόκησα. Luke xii. 32, εὐδόκησεν ὁ Πατὴρ ὑμῶν δοῦναι. Heb. x. 6, ὁλοκαυτώματα ... οὐκ εὐδόκησας. This last is a very unusual one (comp. Psal. li. 18. Sept. εὐδοκήσεις θυσίαν); but it does not interfere with the general principle contended for, that εὐδοκέω is a personal verb, and is always construed with a nominative preceding (expressed or understood) as its subject. *It pleased the Father* therefore would be εὐδόκησεν ὁ Πατὴρ, and this could not properly be followed by an infinitive mood having another subject, πᾶν τὸ πλήρωμα*, especially as the construction in the following verse is altogether at variance with it.

In an amended translation of the passage the sense is complete without the insertion of the words, *of the Godhead :* but a comparison of chap. ii. 9 shews that this is intended ; and it may seem almost necessary to supply it in order to make the passage clear to an ordinary reader.

For the meaning of πλήρωμα, and the Apostle's reason for so using it in writing to a church so sadly infected with philosophical heresy, see Parkhurst in πλήρωμα, x.

It may be worth while to notice Dr. Doddridge's

---

* There is an example in Polybius, I. 8, which may seem to justify this construction: ὥστε τοὺς Συρακουσίους...τότε πάντας ὁμοθυμαδὸν εὐδοκῆσαι στρατηγὸν αὐτῶν ὑπάρχειν Ἱέρωνα. This, I believe, is a singular example of the usage even in Polybius ; and will hardly reconcile any one to such an arrangement of the passage before us, in which there is really no clue to assist us in discovering what is the subject of εὐδόκησε. *The Father* seems nothing but an arbitrary guess.

paraphrase: "*For in him* his Father is ever well pleased, as he declared by a voice from heaven: and *it was his* sovereign *pleasure,* as dwelling in him, to inhabit the whole fulness of the church; and, to qualify him for the high office which he sustains, he hath appointed *that all fulness* of gifts and graces *should* ever *reside* in him, even all the fulness of the Godhead bodily." Could the learned and estimable author persuade himself, that all this was included in the Apostle's words? And of what use is it, on the ground of a supposed ambiguity in a passage, to dilute it with a multitude of words involving contradictory explanations, to the great perplexity of young students?

Ib. 23.   *To every creature which is under heaven.* ἐν πάσῃ τῇ κτίσει τῇ ὑπὸ τὸν οὐρανόν. 'In all the creation under heaven'—equivalent, as Bishop Middleton has remarked, to ἐν παντὶ τῷ κόσμῳ, v. 6.

Ib. 25.   *According to the dispensation of God which is given to me for you, to fulfil the word of God.* (Marg. *fully to preach the word of God.*) κατὰ τὴν οἰκονομίαν τοῦ Θεοῦ τὴν δοθεῖσάν μοι εἰς ὑμᾶς πληρῶσαι τὸν λόγον τοῦ Θεοῦ. 'According to the dispensation of God which is given unto me, to fulfil towards you the word of God.' It seems better to connect εἰς ὑμᾶς with πληρῶσαι than with δοθεῖσάν μοι. Then for the sense of πληρῶσαι with λόγον in this passage and εὐαγγέλιον in Rom. xv. 19, I cannot satisfy myself that it means *fully to preach,* as there rendered in the text and here in the margin. It may better perhaps be referred to the οἰκονομία, expressed here and implied in the other passage, the dispensation or stewardship committed to him, which he was to fulfil by preaching the gospel. See 1 Corinth. ix. 17, and also 2 Tim. iv. 17, πληροφορηθῇ.

But perhaps after all τὴν δοθεῖσάν μοι εἰς ὑμᾶς may have the sense of *reaching as far as you,* like ἄχρι καὶ ὑμῶν, in 2 Cor. x. 13.

ii. 2. *Of God, and of the Father, and of Christ.* τοῦ Θεοῦ καὶ πατρὸς καὶ τοῦ Χριστοῦ. 'Of God and the Father, and of Christ.' The English translation expresses three persons; the original, most distinctly two. Griesbach indeed omits all the words after Θεοῦ, but our Translators have followed the editions which retain them. The sense of the passage being clear from the omission of the Article before πατρὸς, the best way of expressing that sense may still be doubtful; whether as I have done it, or as others, *God even the Father.* I much question the correctness of this latter method, and think that its adoption might lead to serious difficulties in other passages. *Of God and the Father* means, according to all received principles, *Of him who is both God and the Father.* The mystery therefore referred to is, God revealed not merely in the unity of his character, but in the plurality of Persons, the Son as well as the Father—*God in Christ reconciling the world unto himself**.

Ib. 3. *In whom are hid all the treasures of wisdom and knowledge.* ἐν ᾧ εἰσὶ πάντες οἱ θησαυροὶ τῆς σοφίας καὶ τῆς γνώσεως ἀπόκρυφοι. 'Wherein are hid all the treasures

---

* See the note on 1 Corinth. xv. 24.

of wisdom and knowledge.' *Wherein,* or *in which,* i. e. in which mystery. And so the margin. That this is the relation of the pronoun, cannot be doubted. If it were to be understood of a person, it would be uncertain whether it were Christ or the Father. But the whole scope of the passage is placed beyond a question by 1 Corinth. ii. 7, λαλοῦμεν σοφίαν Θεοῦ ἐν μυστηρίῳ τὴν ἀποκεκρυμμένην, which might be rendered with greater simplicity, *the wisdom of God which is hidden in a mystery.*

Ib. 12. *Through the faith of the operation of God.* διὰ τῆς πίστεως τῆς ἐνεργείας τοῦ Θεοῦ. 'Through faith in the operation of God.' So Mark xi. 22, ἔχετε πίστιν Θεοῦ, *have faith in God.*

Ib. 23. *Not in any honour to the satisfying of the flesh.* οὐκ ἐν τιμῇ τινι πρὸς πλησμονὴν τῆς σαρκός. 'Not with any regard—or, not shewing any regard—to the satisfying of the flesh*.'

---

* A new view of this difficult passage has lately been given, which has much to recommend it besides the high station of its Author. The Archbishop of Canterbury in his recently published Exposition of this epistle explains it thus: "These things are of little honour or value *against the fulness of the flesh,* the motions of sin in the members. Πρός, *contra,* as πρὸς κέντρα λακτίζειν: πλησμονὴν, repletion, excess; as Exod. xvi. 5, ἠσθίομεν ἄρτους εἰς πλησμονήν." The only remark I would presume to offer on a rendering which brings out so apposite a sense, is that in such an arrangement—which makes this clause the apodosis to the former—we should certainly have expected δὲ or ἀλλὰ to answer to the preceding μέν; and there seems also a want of simplicity in the expression οὐκ ἐν τιμῇ τινι so understood. But the sense is very forcible: these things had a shew of power and fitness for mortifying the flesh; but in reality they were of no value for that purpose.

iii. 8. *But now ye also put off all these.* νυνὶ δὲ ἀπό_
θεσθε καὶ ὑμεῖς τὰ πάντα. 'But now do ye also lay them
all aside.' The common translation sounds as if intended
to express, *ye do*—whereas it should be imperative, *do
ye*. And there is an emphasis in καὶ ὑμεῖς, *ye also*, who
before walked in them (v. 7). And this leads to another
remark: can ἐν οἷς and ἐν αὐτοῖς, in v. 7, have the same
reference, viz. to the *things* enumerated in v. 5? For
αὐτοῖς indeed there is a various reading, τούτοις, but this
is no improvement. Retaining therefore αὐτοῖς, I would
understand it as referring to τοὺς υἱοὺς τῆς ἀπειθείας, and
render, *when ye lived among them.* Compare Ephes. ii. 3,
ἐν οἷς—ἐν ταῖς ἐπιθυμίαις, where the reference is in an in_
verted order.

To the rendering of ἀπόθεσθε, *put off*, it is a great
objection, that that is the rendering afterwards of ἀπεκ_
δυσάμενοι in v. 9; and it misleads an English reader to
suppose that the same idea is expressed in the two verses.
In a precisely. parallel passage, 1 Pet. ii. 1, ἀποθέμενοι is
rendered *laying aside.* In iii. 21 of the same epistle the
word ἀπόθεσις is translated yet more literally, *putting
away.*

Ib. 11. *Where there is neither Greek nor Jew, circumcision nor uncircumcision, barbarian, Scythian, bond,* nor
free. Ὅπου οὐκ ἔνι Ἕλλην καὶ Ἰουδαῖος, περιτομὴ καὶ ἀκρο-
βυστία, βάρβαρος, Σκύθης, δοῦλος, ἐλεύθερος. 'In which
there is not Greek·and Jew, circumcision and uncircum_
cision, barbarian *and* Scythian, bond *and* free'--i. e. in
which new creation none of these distinctions have an

existence. For the Scythians are opposed to other barbarians as more barbarous, as barbarians in general are opposed to Greeks.

iv. 9. *A faithful.* τῷ πιστῷ. 'The faithful.'

THE

FIRST EPISTLE TO THE THESSALONIANS.

CHAP. i. 10. *Jesus which delivered.* Ἰησοῦν τὸν ῥυόμενον. 'Jesus who delivereth.'

ii. 16. *For the wrath is come upon them.* ἔφθασε δὲ ἐπ' αὐτοὺς ἡ ὀργή. 'And wrath is come upon them.' The clause certainly does not assign a reason for their conduct; but it refers rather to the judgment it was hastening on.

Ib. 20. *For ye are.* ὑμεῖς γάρ ἐστε. 'Verily ye are.' See on Rom. v. 7.

iii. 5. *Lest by some means the tempter have tempted you, and our labour be in vain.* μήπως ἐπείρασεν ὑμᾶς ὁ πειράζων, καὶ εἰς κενὸν γένηται ὁ κόπος ἡμῶν. 'Whether by any means the tempter have tempted you, and *lest* our labour be in vain.' With this interpretation compare Eurip. Phœniss. 91—2, μή τις φαντάζεται, κἀμοὶ ἔλθῃ. With the authorised rendering compare Galat. ii. 2, where however, if our language would admit of it, the other mode of translation would perhaps be more correct.

Ib. 9. *Can we render to God again for you.* δυνάμεθα τῷ Θεῷ ἀνταποδοῦναι περὶ ὑμῶν. 'Can we render to God for you.' The word *again* was intended, I suppose, to be equivalent to *back*, ἀντὶ, but it is not necessary, and conveys a different idea. See chap. i. 6 of the next Epistle.

Ib. 11, 12. *Now God himself and our Father. Before God, even our Father.* αὐτὸς δὲ ὁ Θεὸς καὶ πατὴρ ἡμῶν. ἔμπροσθεν τοῦ Θεοῦ καὶ πατρὸς ἡμῶν. 'But may our God and Father himself.' 'Before our God and Father'—or 'Before God our Father.' See the note on 1 Cor. xv. 24.

iv. 6. *In* any *matter.* ἐν τῷ πράγματι. 'In the matter,' as the margin; viz. the matter of fornication. The error of the common translation, by which the unity of the subject is so palpably violated, is exposed at length in Bishop Middleton's note.

Ib. ib. *Of all such.* περὶ πάντων τούτων. 'For all these things.'

v. 15. *Both among yourselves, and to all* men. καὶ εἰς ἀλλήλους καὶ εἰς πάντας. 'Both towards one another, and towards all *men.*' This is the translation of the same words in chap. iii. 12.

SECOND EPISTLE TO THE THESSALONIANS.

CHAP. i. 11. *Of this calling.* τῆς κλήσεως. 'Of his calling.' Compare Philipp. iii. 14.

ii. 1. *Now we beseech you, brethren, by the coming.* ἐρωτῶμεν δὲ ὑμᾶς, ἀδελφοί, ὑπὲρ τῆς παρουσίας. 'But we beseech you, brethren, concerning the coming.' So Rom.

ix. 27, ὑπὲρ τοῦ Ἰσραὴλ, *concerning Israel*. And though the other sense of ὑπὲρ be an unquestionable one, yet on a consideration of the whole passage, taken in connexion with chap. iv. of the former Epistle, I think it less suitable here. He is going to speak to them on a subject, concerning which they had been troubled: and the connexion with the verses immediately preceding, chap. i. 7—10, is marked by the particle δὲ, *but*. In the next verse strange liberties of criticism have been taken with the ἀπὸ τοῦ νοὸς, with which I am not concerned. If the translation *in mind* be altered at all, I do not see that any greater change is required than *in your mind*.—In v. 3, *a falling away* should of course be, *the falling away;* and *that man of sin*, *the man of sin.*

Ib. 4. *Above all.* ἐπὶ πάντα. 'Against all.'

Ib. 6, 7. *And now ye know what withholdeth, that he might be revealed in his time. For the mystery of iniquity doth already work: only he who now letteth will let, until he be taken out of the way.* καὶ νῦν τὸ κατέχον οἴδατε, εἰς τὸ ἀποκαλυφθῆναι αὐτὸν ἐν τῷ ἑαυτοῦ καιρῷ. τὸ γὰρ μυστήριον ἤδη ἐνεργεῖται τῆς ἀνομίας· μόνον ὁ κατέχων ἄρτι, ἕως ἐκ μέσου γένηται. 'And now ye know what withholdeth *him*, that he may be revealed in his own time. For the mystery of iniquity is already working: only there is *one* that now withholdeth *it*, until he be taken out of the way.' In a passage of such deep interest, and which has been the subject of such multifarious criticism, it is important to make the translation as accurate and perspicuous as possible; and in order to this the participle κατέχων should not be rendered in one verse by *withholdeth,* and in the other by *letteth.* Something is also gained in perspicuity by supplying the accusatives which in the original are omitted after the participles. The loose rendering of ἑαυτοῦ also, *his* instead of *his own,* is far from assisting the clearness of the passage: *that he may be revealed in his own time*—the time appointed for him, and not before. In the clause, μόνον ὁ κατέχων ἄρτι, there is some ambiguity as to the matter to be supplied. It might be as in our version, "he who now letteth *will let;*" but it seems rather harsh to insert so important a supplement without an evident necessity. The construction I have adopted would properly require ἔστιν to be expressed, as in John v. 45, ἔστιν ὁ κατηγορῶν ὑμῶν, *There is* one *that accuseth you;* and viii. 50, ἔστιν ὁ ζητῶν καὶ κρίνων· but the omission may be tolerated.

Ib. 10. *Deceivableness.* ἀπάτη. 'Deceitfulness.' I do not perceive the ground of adopting a different translation, which quite changes the idea.

Ib. 11. *A lie.* τῷ ψεύδει. 'The lie,' viz. of the Apostasy. It might be *falsehood* generally; but if expressed with an Article, it must be the definite one.

Ib. 15. *Whether by word or our epistle.* εἴτε διὰ λόγου εἴτε δι᾽ ἐπιστολῆς ἡμῶν. 'Whether by our word or epistle.' The ἡμῶν belongs to both words, as ἀγαθῷ in the last verse of the chapter belongs to λόγῳ and ἔργῳ.

Ib. 16. *And God, even our Father.* καὶ ὁ Θεὸς καὶ πατὴρ ἡμῶν. 'And God our Father.' See on 1 Corinth. xv. 24, Coloss. ii. 2, and 1 Thess. iii. 11, 13.

iii. 5. *The patient waiting for Christ.* ὑπομονὴν τοῦ Χριστοῦ. 'The patience of Christ,' as the margin; i. e. suffering for him.   Compare Rev. i. 9, ἐν τῇ βασιλείᾳ καὶ ὑπομονῇ Ἰησοῦ Χριστοῦ.

Ib. 14. *By this epistle.* διὰ τῆς ἐπιστολῆς. 'By our epistle.' The article seems to me to be conclusive against connecting the words with τοῦτον σημειοῦσθε:—unless indeed it should be, *by your epistle,* an epistle which they were to write to him.

THE FIRST EPISTLE TO TIMOTHY.

CHAP. i. 18. *A good warfare.* τὴν καλὴν στρατείαν. 'The good warfare,' viz. of faith.   See chap. vi. 12.   So in the 2d Epistle, iv. 7, it should be, *I have fought the good fight:* τὸν ἀγῶνα τὸν καλὸν ἠγώνισμαι.

Ib. 19. *Concerning faith have made shipwreck.* περὶ τὴν πίστιν ἐναυάγησαν. 'Have made shipwreck of the faith.' Literally, *with regard to the faith.*

ii. 4. *Who will have all men to be saved.* ὃς πάντας ἀνθρώπους θέλει σωθῆναι. 'Who willeth that all men should be saved.'

Ib. 6. *To be testified in due time.* τὸ μαρτύριον καιροῖς ἰδίοις. '*Which is* the testimony for his times.' The difficulty of this passage is confessed by all, and is not a little increased by the presence of the Article.   I understand it to mean, that the great fact of Christ's having given

himself a ransom for all, is that which is to be testified
by his servants *in his times,* i. e. in the times of the gospel:
it is to be the great subject of their preaching.   Compare Titus i. 3.   The words καιροῖς ἰδίοις occur in a sense
a little different from this in chap. vi. 15 of this Epistle.

Ib. 15.   See on 1 Pet. iii. 20.

iv. 1, 2.   *Doctrines of devils ; Speaking lies in hypocrisy ;*
having their conscience seared with a hot iron. διδασκαλίαις
δαιμονίων, ἐν ὑποκρίσει ψευδολόγων, κεκαυτηριασμένων τὴν
ἰδίαν συνείδησιν.   'Doctrines of dæmons, Through the hypocrisy of liars, who have their own conscience seared
with a hot iron.'   If the construction followed by our
Translators be admitted, of course ψευδολόγων must agree
with δαιμονίων, whereas their translation unquestionably
conveys to an English reader the idea that it agrees with
τινὲς, the persons who *depart :* even on this ground therefore some correction is absolutely necessary.   And few,
I think, will doubt after a full consideration of the passage, that nothing less will do than that which I have
adopted, which clears up the whole construction by introducing a term to which the following genitives may
be referred; whereas otherwise they must have belonged
somehow or other to δαιμονίων, the subject of the heresy,
when the sense of the whole shews that they belong to
the heretics themselves.—I have given the strong sense,
their own, to ἰδίαν, as intimating that, their own conscience
being seared, they have no compunction in destroying the
souls of others.

Ib. 15.   *Meditate upon these things.*   ταῦτα μελέτα.   'Εxercise thyself in these things.' *Meditate* is certainly too confined. In Psalm i. 2, the word which is translated *meditate* is rendered in the Septuagint μελετήσει, and accordingly is translated in the Prayer-Book, *exercise himself*. A good illustration of the word is the manner in which Thucydides frequently uses it; ex. gr. I. 142, where he speaks of the Athenians having obtained their naval pre-eminence by *long training and practice:* μελετῶντες αὐτὸ εὐθὺς ἀπὸ τῶν Μηδικῶν.—At the end of the verse I prefer the marginal reading, *in all things; ἐν πᾶσι.* See Coloss. i. 18. Titus ii. 10. Hebrews xiii. 18. 1 Pet. iv. 11.

v. 4. *Or nephews.* ἢ ἔκγονα. 'Or descendants.' The word *nephews* in its old sense is not now understood.

Ib. 11. *For when they have begun to wax wanton against Christ, they will marry.* ὅταν γὰρ καταστρηνιάσωσι τοῦ Χριστοῦ, γαμεῖν θέλουσιν. 'For when they grow wanton against Christ, they desire to marry.'

vi. 2. *Because they are faithful* (marg. *believing*) *and beloved, partakers of the benefit.* ὅτι πιστοί εἰσι καὶ ἀγαπητοὶ οἱ τῆς εὐεργεσίας ἀντιλαμβανόμενοι. 'Because they who partake of *their* service are believing and beloved.' Literally, *who partake of the benefit.* And this might do, if understood to mean, *of the benefit of their service.* The common translation cannot stand, unless the article οἱ be expunged: and even then τῆς εὐεργεσίας could hardly mean, *the benefit* of the gospel.—The sense here given to ἀντιλαμβανόμενοι is certainly unusual: but see Euseb. Hist. Eccl. v. 15, εὐωδίας τοσαύτης ἀντελαμβανόμεθα. Or it might be rendered here, 'Who lay claim to *their* service.'

Ib. 3. *To wholesome words,* even *the words of our Lord.* ὑγιαίνουσι λόγοις τοῖς τοῦ Κυρίου ἡμῶν. 'To the sound words of our Lord.' *Sound words* is, I believe, every where else the translation given of ὑγιαίνοντες λόγοι.

Ib. 5. *That gain is godliness.* πορισμὸν εἶναι τὴν εὐσέβειαν. 'That godliness is gain.' The Article before εὐσέβειαν shews unquestionably that it is to precede the verb.

Ib. 12. *Hast professed a good profession.* ὡμολόγησας τὴν καλὴν ὁμολογίαν. 'Hast made the good confession.' So, in the next v. *witnessed the good confession.* The substantive is the same in both cases, and should therefore convey that idea to an English reader: in both cases also the definite Article has an emphasis which ought by all means to be retained: *the good confession* of the gospel.

In vv. 7, 14, *this world, this commandment* should be *the world, the commandment.*

Ib. 13. *And* before *Christ Jesus.* καὶ Χριστοῦ Ἰησοῦ. 'And *of* Christ Jesus.' The alteration shews, that *Christ Jesus* is in the same construction as *God* preceding, and also avoids the inelegant repetition of the word *before.*

THE SECOND EPISTLE TO TIMOTHY.

CHAP. i. 9. *According to his own purpose and grace, which was given us.* κατ' ἰδίαν πρόθεσιν, καὶ χάριν τὴν δοθεῖσαν ἡμῖν. 'According to his own purpose and the grace which was given us.' I think it plain that δοθεῖσαν belongs only to χάριν, and then χάριν τὴν δοθεῖσαν must be rendered in English the same as if it were τὴν χάριν τὴν δ.

Ib. 13. *Hold fast the form of sound words, which thou hast heard of me, in faith and love.* ὑποτύπωσιν ἔχε ὑγιαινόντων λόγων, ὧν παρ' ἐμοῦ ἤκουσας, ἐν πίστει καὶ ἀγάπῃ. 'Keep the form of the sound words, which thou heardest from me, in faith and love.' (*Outline* would be more accurate than *form;* but the word seems hardly to harmonize with the character of our version.) So in ver. 2 of the next chapter, ἃ ἤκουσας παρ' ἐμοῦ διὰ πολλῶν μαρτύρων. Connecting the two passages together, and considering the tense in which the Apostle expresses the fact, must we not understand him to refer, not to his general teaching—what Timothy had heard from him throughout his whole intercourse with him, but to what he had heard from him on some one particular occasion? And we have intimations elsewhere of such lessons inculcated on him at the solemn season of his ordination; when upon his making the good confession (1 Tim. vi. 12) he received from the apostle the *deposit*—the *good deposit* —of the sound doctrine he was to preach (τὴν καλὴν παρακαταθήκην, 1 Tim. vi. 20, and 2 Tim. i. 14.)

ii. 3. *Endure hardness.* κακοπάθησον. 'Endure affliction.' Rendered in Chap. iv. 5, *endure afflictions.* Timothy seems to have been a man of a tender spirit, as well as of weak health. See 1 Tim. v. 23. 2 Tim. i. 4, 7, 8, &c. 1 Corinth. xvi. 10.

Ib. 4. *No man that warreth.* οὐδεὶς στρατευόμενος. 'No man engaged in warfare,' or, 'no man serving as a soldier.'

Ib. 5. *And if a man also strive for masteries.* ἐὰν δὲ καὶ ἀθλῇ τις. 'And if a man also contend in the games.' And much more should the same correction be applied to 1 Corinth. ix. 25, where the very word ἀγὼν is expressly included in the participle ἀγωνιζόμενος.

Ib. 26. *And that they may recover themselves out of the snare of the devil, who are taken captive by him at his will.* καὶ ἀνανήψωσιν ἐκ τῆς τοῦ διαβόλου παγίδος, ἐζωγρημένοι ὑπ' αὐτοῦ, εἰς τὸ ἐκείνου θέλημα. 'And having been led captive by the devil, they may recover themselves out of his snare, to *do* the will of God.' I assume that no one is satisfied with the authorised version here. To suppose that the two pronouns αὐτοῦ and ἐκείνου in the same sentence refer to the same person, involves a harshness to which I think nothing would reconcile us but our un-happy familiarity with a wrong translation. The attempt of Scultetus to vindicate it only provokes a smile: "Maluit autem dicere ἐκείνου quam repetere αὐτοῦ, quod legenti ingratum fuisset!"—In Luke ix. 34, αὐτοὺς and ἐκείνους *appear* to refer to the same persons, (at least in our translation,) viz. the three disciples, Peter, James, and John: but a little consideration will convince any one that ἐκείνους must be understood of Moses and Elias; and the disciples might well fear when they saw the cloud put out of sight and take away those whom they had thought of placing on an equality with the Lord himself.

In the proposed translation ἐκείνου is made to refer to ὁ Θεὸς in the preceding verse. It was necessary in trans-lating to repeat the noun itself instead of the pronoun *his*, in order to avoid the confusion which would have arisen from expressing both αὐτοῦ and ἐκείνου by the same English word.   This liberty, which is not too great to be justified by the necessity of the case, our Translators have taken in two instances, where the necessity was by no means urgent. See John vii. 50, and xiii. 6, with the margin of each*.

The rendering of εἰς τὸ θέλημα, to do, &c. is only the use of that pregnant sense of this preposition, which is common in the writings of St Paul.   The example most exactly to the point is Romans xiii. 14, εἰς ἐπιθυμίας, to fulfil the lusts.   Comp. also Rom. i. 5; vi. 16, 19, &c.

iii. 11.   Persecutions, afflictions, which came unto me at Antioch. τοῖς διωγμοῖς, τοῖς παθήμασιν, οἷά μοι ἐγένετο ἐν Ἀντιοχείᾳ. 'Persecutions, afflictions; what afflictions came to me at Antioch.'   It is clear that by οἷα is meant οἷα παθήματα, just as οἵους διωγμοὺς immediately follows: and as διωγμοὺς is repeated in the one clause, παθήματα must be understood in the other, that the proper force of οἷα may be preserved.—Some perhaps may prefer, 'What things happened unto me.'

iv. 7.   See on 1 Tim. i. 18.

Ib. 8.   A crown of righteousness. ὁ τῆς δικαιοσύνης στέφανος. 'The crown of righteousness.'   The emphasis in such expressions is clearly important.   So in Revel. ii. 10.

Ib. 20.   At Miletum. ἐν Μιλήτῳ. 'At Miletus.'

* On Thucyd. I. 132. παιδικά ποτε ὢν αὐτοῦ καὶ πιστότατος ἐκείνῳ, Poppo remarks: "Noli mirari hæc pronomina de eodem (sc. Pausania) dicta esse." But I cannot agree with the learned annotator in his opinion: it seems much more natural to understand the two pronouns of the two persons already mentioned, the αὐτοῦ referring to Artabazus, and the ἐκείνῳ to Pausanias.   The passages which Poppo refers to, IV. 29, VI. 61, to bear out his view, appear to me unsuitable.

THE EPISTLE TO TITUS.

CHAP. i. 6. *Not accused of riot or unruly.* μη ἐν κατ-
ηγορίᾳ ἀσωτίας ἢ ἀνυπότακτα. 'Who are not chargeable
with riot, or unruly.' We may venture to supply *who are*,
for the sake of avoiding ambiguity.

Ib. 9. *Holding fast the faithful word as he hath been
taught.* (Marg. *in teaching.*) ἀντεχόμενον τοῦ κατὰ τὴν δι-
δαχὴν πιστοῦ λόγου. 'Holding fast the faithful word
according to the doctrine.' The common translation may
be justified; but the marginal rendering is altogether
indefensible.

Ib. ib. *That he may be able by sound doctrine both to
exhort and to convince the gainsayers.* ἵνα δυνατὸς ᾖ καὶ πα-
ρακαλεῖν ἐν τῇ διδασκαλίᾳ τῇ ὑγιαινούσῃ, καὶ τοὺς ἀντιλέγοντας
ἐλέγχειν. 'That he may be able both to exhort *men* by
sound doctrine, and to convince gainsayers.' The arrangement in the common translation makes the gainsayers
dependent on both the verbs, *exhort* and *convince;* whereas
the order of the words in the original studiously shews the
contrary. And as the *exhortation* mentioned is generally
descriptive of the work of preaching, I have ventured
to insert *men*, in order to remove all ambiguity.—In
English *gainsayers* without the Article, marking a class of
persons, is equivalent to the Greek expression, where the
Article is properly inserted.

Ib. 10. *For there are many unruly and vain talkers.*
εἰσὶ γὰρ πολλοὶ καὶ ἀνυπότακτοι ματαιολόγοι. 'For there are

many unruly vain talkers.' The καὶ of the original is merely pleonastic after πολλοὶ, indicating that the vain talkers are both *many* and *unruly* : but the English copula expresses that they are both *unruly talkers* and *vain talkers.*

ii. 13. *Looking for that blessed hope, and the glorious appearing of the great God and our Saviour Jesus Christ:* προσδεχόμενοι τὴν μακαρίαν ἐλπίδα, καὶ ἐπιφάνειαν τῆς δόξης τοῦ μεγάλου Θεοῦ καὶ σωτῆρος ἡμῶν Ἰησοῦ Χριστοῦ. 'Looking for the blessed hope, and the glorious appearing of our great God and Saviour Jesus Christ.' When our Translators render the definite Article by *this* or *that,* (see on Matt. xv. 12. Acts xix. 9,) they sometimes print it in Italics, to mark its absence from the original, and sometimes not. By adopting such a translation of τὴν in the present passage, they make it point immediately and definitely to the ἐπιφάνεια following as the object of the hope ; on which account they ought, *on their own principles,* (see on 2 Thessal. ii. 16, and also on Coloss. ii. 2,) to have rendered καὶ *even.* According to the literal translation, *the blessed hope* must be considered as a general expression for the hope and expectation of all believers, and *the glorious appearing* as subjoined to point to the time of the consummation of their hope. Compare Acts xxiii. 6, περὶ ἐλπίδος καὶ ἀναστάσεως νεκρῶν.——If any one were to contend that the absence of τὴν before ἐπιφάνειαν must so closely connect it with ἐλπίδα, as to require a more literal rendering, *the blessed hope and appearing of the glory of*—this would open a new question.

In the remaining words the Article inserted before Θεοῦ and omitted before σωτῆρος marks the two substantives as designating the same person, and also that ἡμῶν depends on both of them. See on Ephes. v. 5.

iii. 8. This is *a faithful saying, and these things I will that thou affirm constantly.* πιστὸς ὁ λόγος· καὶ περὶ τούτων βούλομαί σε διαβεβαιοῦσθαι. 'It *is* a faithful saying, and concerning these things I will that thou affirm constantly.' —The words πιστὸς ὁ λόγος occur several times in St Paul's writings; 1 Tim. i. 15, iii. 1. 2 Tim. ii. 11. In the last-mentioned passage, our Translators have rendered them as I here propose. This comes a little nearer to the literal sense, which is, *The saying* is *faithful;* and on that account I prefer it here, because the meaning of the verse is matter of dispute, and therefore in settling it it is important to have the advantage of the greatest possible exactness of translation. On the same ground, but with much stronger reason, I think it important to preserve the literal rendering of περὶ τούτων.—The two interpretations between which the dispute lies, are as follows: 'Affirm these things, viz. that believers maintain good works;' in which case good works are directly enjoined: and, 'the doctrine I have mentioned in the preceding vv. of salvation by the mercy of God in Christ, is a faithful and true saying, and I would have you constantly insist upon it and preach about it, in order that believers may maintain good works;' in which case good works are secured as the necessary consequence of the doctrine preached.— The new translation of περὶ τούτων will go in favour, perhaps, of the latter interpretation; but if any one think that an argument on the same side can be grounded on the general sense of ἵνα with a subjunctive, he must carefully examine the usage of the New Testament, and may compare among other passages Matthew xxviii. 10; Mark vi. 12; 1 John iii. 2, v. 16; 2 John, 6. Our Translators seem to have intended to hold the balance between the two interpretations by the use of the word *might* (*might be careful*), which, if the meaning of the passage were certainly settled, would require either to be altered to may, or to be omitted altogether.—A similar ambiguity occurs in 1 John ii. 1, though there I consider it nearly certain, that the sense of ἵνα is, *in order that*.

Ibid. *These things are good and profitable unto men.* ταῦτά ἐστι τὰ καλὰ καὶ ὠφέλιμα τοῖς ἀνθρώποις. 'These are the things which are good and profitable unto men.' Bishop Middleton says, "I do not perceive the force of the Article: many of the best MSS. omit it." If retained, it must have the force I have given it above.

THE EPISTLE TO PHILEMON.

V. 21. *I wrote unto thee.* ἔγραψά σοι. 'I have written unto thee;' as it is translated in v. 19. The Apostle is certainly not speaking of a former Epistle. See on 1 Corinth. v. 9.

THE EPISTLE TO THE HEBREWS.

CHAP. ii. 9. *But we see Jesus, who was made a little lower than the angels, for the suffering of death, crowned with glory and honour; that he by the grace of God should taste death for every man.* τὸν δὲ βραχύ τι παρ' ἀγγέλους ἠλαττωμένον βλέπομεν Ἰησοῦν διὰ τὸ πάθημα τοῦ θανάτου δόξῃ καὶ τιμῇ ἐστεφανωμένον, ὅπως χάριτι Θεοῦ ὑπὲρ παντὸς γεύσηται θανάτου. 'But Jesus, who was made a little lower than the angels for the suffering of death, that by the grace of God he might taste death for every man, we see crowned with glory and honour.' The object of this transposition is to shew, that the clause, ὅπως—θανάτου, is merely exegetical of διὰ τὸ πάθημα τοῦ θανάτου, *for the purpose of suffering death.* There is indeed a slight inconvenience in the transposition, because the 10th verse clearly assigns a reason why Jesus should so have suffered, and this connexion was marked by the insertion of the clause ὅπως—θανάτου at the end of the former verse: but it seems desirable to admit this inconvenience in order to get rid of the more serious difficulty arising from the interposition of δόξῃ καὶ τιμῇ ἐστεφανωμένον between the two clauses relating to the suffering; a difficulty which is felt in the Greek, but much more in the English. (Beza adopts a different transposition for the same purpose, viz. 'But we see Jesus crowned with glory and honour, who'—)—For the sense here given to διὰ, *for the purpose of,* having reference to a future result, compare Rom. iii. 25, and

9

iv. 25.   The marginal rendering of βραχύ τι, *a little while*, introduces an incongruity not to be tolerated; being a sense utterly inadmissible in the Psalm quoted (the eighth), where the object is to give the most exalted view of man in his creation, as being *only* a little lower than the angels.

Ib. 11.   *For both he that sanctifieth and they who are sanctified.*   ὅ τε γὰρ ἁγιάζων καὶ οἱ ἁγιαζόμενοι.   'For both the purifier and the purified.'   The passages in which ἁγιάζω occurs in this epistle, besides the present, are the following: ix. 13; x. 10, 14, 29; xiii. 12.   From a careful inspection of these passages every one must feel the difficulty of retaining the common rendering of ἁγιάζω, *sanctify*, in its proper and ordinary sense of *making holy*. This will be felt especially in chap. x. 10 and 29.

Again, it will evidently appear in some of these passages, that there is a close affinity in sense between ἁγιάζω and καθαρίζω.   For example, in chap. ix. 13, 14, εἰ ... ἁγιάζει πρὸς τὴν τῆς σαρκὸς καθαρότητα, πόσῳ μᾶλλον ... καθαριεῖ τὴν συνείδησιν ὑμῶν...; And this latter word is generally expressed by *purging* or *purifying* : see chap. i. 3 ; ix. 22, 23 ; x. 2.

Now, whereas καθαρίζω is more immediately connected with *justification*, which includes cleansing from sin, washing it away and removing its guilt, and so accounting righteous; and ἁγιάζω, in its ordinary usage, expresses *sanctification*, the removal of the power of sin, and making holy; a consideration of this general distinction in connexion with all the passages above referred to will prepare us to admit a modified sense of ἀγιάζω, one more allied to that of καθαρίζω, throughout this remarkable epistle. Nor is it difficult to suggest a reason why it should be so. The epistle itself possesses a character of its own—is addressed to Jews—is mainly on the subject of the καθαρισμοὶ of the Jewish law; and, above all, is written by one, and to others, who were familiar with all the terms of that law in the Hebrew language. Now it has been well observed that ἀγιάζω is the word made use of by the LXX. Translators to express the Hebrew קָדַשׁ, and the manner in which that word is frequently employed in the original, and translated by the LXX., shews that it bore a much wider sense than we attach to the term *sanctify*. Compare among other passages Exod. xxix. 33, 36, with the Sept. translation. This modified sense of ἀγιάζω will add much to the perspicuity of the different passages.

iii. 16. *For some, when they had heard, did provoke: howbeit not all that came out of Egypt by Moses.* τινὲς γὰρ ἀκούσαντες παρεπίκραναν, ἀλλ᾽ οὐ πάντες οἱ ἐξελθόντες ἐξ Αἰγύπτου διὰ Μωσέως. (But Griesbach reads, τίνες—παρεπίκραναν ;—Μωσέως;) 'For who after they had heard provoked? did not all who had come out of Egypt by Moses?' So the ἀλλὰ will be redundant, nearly answering to our idiom, *Why, did not*— Or if a comma only be placed at παρεπίκραναν, render, 'For who, &c. but all who—' in which case οὐ is nearly redundant, two forms of expression being in a manner blended together.

iv. 2. *For unto us was the gospel preached as well as unto them: but the word preached did not profit them.* καὶ γάρ ἐσμεν εὐηγγελισμένοι καθάπερ κἀκεῖνοι· ἀλλ' οὐκ ὠφέλησεν ὁ λόγος τῆς ἀκοῆς ἐκείνους. 'For we have the glad tidings *thereof,* even as they; but the word of *its* report (or, the word which they heard) did not profit them.' The common translation seems quite unintelligible. The clause, *Unto us was the gospel preached,* suggests the question, When? There is doubtless an allusion to the gospel in the passage, inasmuch as the Apostle's argument sets forth *rest* (the rest of Canaan and the rest of heaven) as the great promise of both dispensations: but it is neither the GOSPEL, strictly speaking, nor *preaching* as the method of making it known, which is here referred to. It is *the promise of entering into his rest:* and as this promise was theirs in type, it is ours as well as theirs in substance. It follows therefore:

Ib. 3. *For we which have believed do enter into rest.* εἰσερχόμεθα γὰρ εἰς τὴν κατάπαυσιν οἱ πιστεύσαντες. 'For we who have believed enter into the rest'—i. e. the rest promised, v. 1. And, *all* who believe; we as well as they. It is expressed in the present tense, as being not a past action, like their entering into Canaan, but an action continually going on. The common notion, which supposes it to mean that faith gives a present foretaste of heaven, seems to me to be quite out of place.

Ib. 8. *Jesus.* Ἰησοῦς. 'Joshua.' Whether such a rendering as that proposed would be consistent with the duty of a faithful translator, may perhaps be questioned. But it is to be considered that our translation after all is made for English readers, the great bulk of whom never enter into the bearings of the question about the different languages in which the different parts were written; and consequently are hopelessly perplexed about the assertion here made of Jesus. The son of Nun is known to them only by the name of Joshua: it is really a hard lesson for them to learn and reduce to practical use, that Joshua is the same name with Jesus; the difference between Jehoram and Joram, and other similar instances, is nothing to it. As a practical question therefore, in which the spiritual welfare of millions is more or less concerned, it may be worth while to consider whether the change would not be justifiable; especially as it would occasion no perplexity to those who understand the principles of the respective formations of the two words from different languages.—These remarks apply also, though with less force, to Acts vii. 45.

Ib. 10. *For he that is entered into his rest, he also hath ceased from his own works, as God did from his.* ὁ γὰρ εἰσελθὼν εἰς τὴν κατάπαυσιν αὐτοῦ, καὶ αὐτὸς κατέπαυσεν ἀπὸ τῶν ἔργων αὐτοῦ, ὥσπερ ἀπὸ τῶν ἰδίων ὁ Θεός. 'For he that is entered into his rest hath himself also rested from his works, as God *did* from his own.' This is certainly more literal than the authorised version; and the change may give us a little assistance towards understanding the difficult argument. Let us look then to the *nexus orationis*.

The main sentence, on which the rest of the passage is dependent, is contained in vv. 6, 11: *Seeing therefore it remaineth that some must enter therein, and they to whom it was first preached* (or, *promised*) *entered not in because of unbelief; Let us labour therefore to enter into that rest, lest any man fall after the same example of unbelief.* But four verses, 7—10, are interposed as a parenthesis, the object of which is to establish the statement which he had laid down as the basis of the exhortation of v. 11: and this part of the argument, being somewhat obscure from the abrupt style of the Apostle, may be made clearer by a paraphrase: v. 7, 'And this fact of the promised rest not having been yet bestowed is still more evident from God's *fixing a certain day so long after* the entrance into Canaan, and saying in the psalm, *To-day if ye will hear,* &c. *For* (v. 8), *if Joshua had given them rest,* and the rest of Canaan had been the antitype which contained the final accomplishment of the promise instead of being itself a type of something yet to come, God *would not have spoken of another day after this. So then,* v. 9, *there remaineth a rest* or sabbath-keeping *to the people of God,* which shall more exactly and fully complete the type of the original rest, when God kept sabbath (שָׁבַת) from all his work which he created and made. And this is that declared in the gospel: *for* according to it *he that is entered into his rest* (Jesus, as our forerunner) *himself also rested from his works as God did from his own.*'

So far as the promise related only generally to rest, Canaan was a fulfilment of it: but the antitype of God's resting after the work of creation is found only in Jesus, who entered into his rest when by his resurrection he rested from the work of the second creation. And the analogy holds more perfectly in another respect, viz. that in each case the person resting is God.

This view contains only an indirect argument, but that a very strong one, for the change of the day of the sabbath from the last to the first of the week. The second creation takes precedence of the first in its claim to the weekly commemoration of the Christian church. See Dr Owen on the passage.

Ib. 13. *That is not manifest in his sight.* ἀφανὴς ἐνώπιον αὐτοῦ. 'That is not manifest before it'—i. e. before the word of God*: and it is just possible that our translators intended *his sight* to refer to the same thing, *his* being used for *its*. At all events the word of God seems to be the subject of this clause, as of the whole preceding verse; and that, the written word, not the Word that "was made flesh:" for it is only St John who applies that name to the Son of God. And in accordance with this view it might be better to render κριτικὸς in v. 12, *able to discern* than *a discerner.*—In the next clause there is an evident transition from the word to its divine Author; and the altered reference of αὐτοῦ is made clear by what follows, πρὸς ὃν, &c.

v. 7. *In that he feared.* ἀπὸ τῆς εὐλαβείας. 'For *his* piety,' as in the margin. And such is no doubt the *meaning* of the version in the text, where *in that* has the force of *inasmuch as:* but since Dr Doddridge, after Dr Whitby,

---

* It is objected that ἐνώπιον is used only in connexion with persons: but see Rev. vii. 15, ἐνώπιον τοῦ θρόνου. It might be added, that the *word* is here introduced as possessing in a manner the attributes of a person.

contends for a different interpretation, which I do not
think the original can bear, viz. *was heard in* being
delivered from *that which he particularly feared;* and since
the same view has been adopted by others also; I have
thought it right to record my opinion in favour of the
sense which is more clearly expressed by the marginal
reading.—ἀπὸ, *for* or *on account of,* Matt. xiii. 44. Luke
xxi. 26. John xxi. 6. Acts xii. 14.

v. 12.   *Ye have need that one teach you again which* be
the first principles of the oracles of God.   πάλιν χρείαν ἔχετε
τοῦ διδάσκειν ὑμᾶς τίνα (τινα) τὰ στοιχεῖα τῆς ἀρχῆς τῶν
λογίων τοῦ Θεοῦ.   'Ye have need that one teach you again
the first principles of the oracles of God.'   This rendering
requires the omission of the accent usually placed upon
τίνα, and which if retained makes a construction incapable,
I think, of being vindicated.   It will be observed that the
authorised version is really a translation of, τοῦ (τινα)
διδάσκειν ὑμᾶς τίνα—This of course cannot be allowed.
Again, Griesbach and others put a comma at ὑμᾶς, thus
introducing a strange and unheard of construction, τοῦ
διδάσκειν ὑμᾶς, without any subject to διδάσκειν.   Some get
over this by supplying τοῦ (ἡμᾶς) διδάσκειν ὑμᾶς, accounting, I suppose, for the omission of the ἡμᾶς on Scultetus's
principle (see on 1 Tim. ii. 26), that "legenti ingratum
fuisset:" but neither this, nor any other principle that I
am aware of, will reconcile us to such an usage.—The
construction which I follow is, τοῦ τινα διδάσκειν ὑμᾶς τὰ
στοιχεῖα—instructing you *in* the principles, not, teaching
you which or what they be.

Ib. 14. *To discern both good and evil.* πρὸς διάκρισιν καλοῦ τε καὶ κακοῦ. 'To discern good and evil.' The τε is correctly inserted in the original; but the idiom of our language does not admit of its retention.

vi. 7. *By whom.* δι' οὕς. 'For whom,' as in the margin, is unquestionably right.

Ib. 20. *Whither the forerunner is for us entered.* ὅπου πρόδρομος ὑπὲρ ἡμῶν εἰσῆλθεν 'Ιησοῦς. 'Whither Jesus is entered *as* a forerunner for us.'

vii. 3. *Without descent.* ἀγενεαλόγητος. 'Without record of descent.' The other translation does not express all the ideas contained in the original word.

Ib. 5. *And verily they that are of the sons of Levi, who receive the office of the priesthood.* καὶ οἱ μὲν ἐκ τῶν υἱῶν Λευὶ τὴν ἱερατείαν λαμβάνοντες. 'And they indeed of the sons of Levi who receive the office of the priesthood.'

Ib. 19. *But the bringing in of a better hope did.* ἐπεισαγωγὴ δὲ κρείττονος ἐλπίδος. 'But *was* the bringing in of a better hope.' This also is the marginal reading; and while it makes the sense much clearer in the English, it seems to me to be required by the syntax of the Greek.

Ib. 22. *Testament.* διαθήκης. 'Covenant.' See on chap. ix. 15—17.

viii. 4. *He should not be a priest.* οὐδ' ἂν ἦν ἱερεύς. 'He would not be a priest at all.' Literally, 'He would not even be.'

Ib. 5. *Who serve unto the example and shadow of heavenly things.* οἵτινες ὑποδείγματι καὶ σκιᾷ λατρεύουσι τῶν ἐπουρανίων. 'Who serve the pattern and shadow of heavenly things;' just as in chap. xiii. 10, οἱ τῇ σκηνῇ λατρεύοντες is translated *who serve the tabernacle*, which is *the pattern and shadow* here meant. Compare chap. ix. 23.

ix. 1. *A worldly sanctuary.* τὸ ἅγιον κοσμικόν. 'The holy furniture.' In the common version each of the three words is wrongly translated. Both ἅγιον and κοσμικὸν being adjectives, one of them must be taken substantively; and the position of the Article determines that that one must be κοσμικόν.—I need not inform the learned reader, that the translation here adopted is borrowed from Bishop Middleton, to whose excellent note on the passage I beg to refer.

Ib. 2. *For there was a tabernacle made, the first, ... which is called the sanctuary.* σκηνὴ γὰρ κατεσκευάσθη ἡ πρώτη, ... ἥτις λέγεται ἁγία (Griesb. ἅγια, other copies, τὰ ἅγια or ἅγια ἁγίων.) 'For there was made the first tabernacle, ... which is called holy.' Two separate questions have here to be considered: whether ἁγία (singular) or ἅγια (plural) be the correct reading in this verse; and whether in the verse following ἅγια ἁγίων, or ἁγία ἁγίων. Editors, who differ in the former verse, generally agree to print ἅγια ἁγίων in the latter: the accuracy of this is matter for consideration. The passage which forms the basis of the whole question is Exod. xxvi. 33: "The veil shall divide unto you between the holy *place* and the most holy." The original is, בֵּין הַקֹּדֶשׁ וּבֵין קֹדֶשׁ הַקֳּדָשִׁים. The Septuagint translation, ἀναμέσον τοῦ ἁγίου καὶ ἀναμέσον τοῦ ἁγίου τῶν ἁγίων. This is literal; and so is our own popular rendering, *The holy of holies*. Not so ἅγια ἁγίων, which would literally be *the holies of holies;* of which it may well be doubted whether it can be justified on any grammatical principles. The meaning of the phrase is that expressed above, *the most holy;* and this superlative sense, according to the Hebrew usage, may be enunciated either by employing the plural for the singular, as in v. 12, εἰς τὰ ἅγια, which should be rendered *into the most holy* place (as in v. 8, τὴν τῶν ἁγίων ὁδὸν = τὴν εἰς τὰ ἅγια ὁδὸν, *the way into the holiest of all:* compare chap. x. 19, παῤῥησίαν εἰς τὴν εἴσοδον τῶν ἁγίων, *boldness to enter into the holiest;*) or by repeating the word in the genitive case, as ἁγία ἁγίων, *the holy of holies:* compare Daniel ix. 24, where the Septuagint again has, ἅγιον ἁγίων. If this view be correct, the form ἅγια ἁγίων, *sancta* sanctorum, will be a combination of the two superlative expressions, and on that ground, I conceive, quite inadmissible.—The reason of the gender here, ἁγία ἁγίων, in place of the ἁγίου ἁγίων of the Septuagint, is clearly its relation to σκηνή: the first σκηνὴ was called ἁγία, *holy;* the second, within the veil, ἁγία ἁγίων, *most holy.* And it seems desirable that an uniform rendering should be preserved throughout: *most holy,* rather than *holiest, holiest of all.* See v. 3, 8, and ch. x. 19.

Ib. 6. *Now when these things were thus ordained, the priests went always into the first tabernacle, accomplishing the service* of God. τούτων δὲ οὕτω κατεσκευασμένων, εἰς μὲν τὴν πρώτην σκηνὴν διαπαντὸς εἰσίασιν οἱ ἱερεῖς τὰς λατρείας ἐπιτελοῦντες. 'Now these things being thus made, the priests go always into the first tabernacle, accomplishing *their* services.' So v. 7 must be corrected, 'goeth the high priest,' 'which he offereth;' and v. 9, 'which *is* a figure for the present time, in which are offered . . . . that cannot make him that doeth the service.' So v. 25 is correctly rendered, 'the high priest entereth,' chap. x. 1, 'can never,' ib. 11, 'the high priest standeth.' The obvious reason of its being expressed in the present tense is, that the Levitical services and sacrifices were still going on at the time the epistle was written.

Ib. 9. *In which.* καθ' ὅν. 'During which.'

Ib. 10. *And carnal ordinances.* (Marg. *rites* or *ceremonies.*) δικαιώμασι σαρκός. 'Justifications of the flesh'— i. e. mere ceremonial cleansing, which could not make the offerer clean *as pertaining to the conscience* (v. 9): in opposition to which Christ, the true sacrifice, is said in v. 14, to *purge the* CONSCIENCE *from dead works.* Compare for the sense v. 13, πρὸς τὴν τῆς σαρκὸς καθαρότητα, and for the use of δικαίωμα Rom. v. 16.

Ib. 11. *By a greater.* διὰ τῆς μείζονος. 'By the greater' —viz. that which he calls in chap. viii. 2, *the true tabernacle,* in opposition, as here, to the shadowy one of Moses.

Ib. 12. *He entered in once into the holy place.* εἰσῆλθεν ἐφάπαξ εἰς τὰ ἅγια. 'Is entered once for all into the most holy *place.*' See on v. 2.

Ib. 15—17. We are now arrived at a passage, perhaps, the most perplexing in the whole of the New Testament. The grand question, upon which the difficulty turns, is, whether διαθήκη is to be understood of a *covenant* or a *testament*. In chap. vii. 22, as we have seen, it is rendered *testament*. (So also in Matthew xxvi. 28.) All through the 8th chapter it is *covenant*. In v. 4 of the present chapter again it is expressed by *covenant;* and then, in the argument contained in the verses now before us, it is changed back to *testament*—of course in the sense of *a will*. Compare especially chap. xii. 24. Waiving the question, whether the more general term *dispensation* do or do not better express the meaning of the word, our present inquiry is, under what particular form, whether *a testament* or *a covenant*, we are to regard the dispensation, so as to comprehend rightly the Apostle's argument in this place. After a long and anxious consideration of the passage, I come to the conclusion that the word ought to be rendered *covenant*, though I am aware of great and serious difficulties in the way of this interpretation, which, I think, are not removed by any thing I have yet seen on the subject*. The passage is as follows:

And for this cause he is the mediator of the new testament, that by means of death, for the redemption of the transgressions that were under the first testament, they which are called might receive the promise of eternal inheritance. For where a testament is, there must also of necessity be the

---

* The Reader may find the arguments on both sides in a discussion of the passage which appeared in the *Christian Observer* for 1820--21. The letters of Mr Faber in favour of the translation I adopt are strongly marked by the clear, straight-forward, sound sense which distinguish that gentleman's writings; though he has left, as I have intimated, some weak points.

*death of the testator.   For a testament is of force after men
are dead : otherwise it is of no strength at all while the testator liveth.*

καὶ διὰ τοῦτο διαθήκης καινῆς μεσίτης ἐστὶν, ὅπως θανάτου
γενομένου εἰς ἀπολύτρωσιν τῶν ἐπὶ τῇ πρώτῃ διαθήκῃ παρα-
βάσεων, τὴν ἐπαγγελίαν λάβωσιν οἱ κεκλημένοι τῆς αἰωνίου
κληρονομίας.

ὅπου γὰρ διαθήκη, θάνατον ἀνάγκη φέρεσθαι τοῦ διαθεμένου.

διαθήκη γὰρ ἐπὶ νεκροῖς βεβαία· ἐπεὶ μήποτε ἰσχύει ὅτε
ζῇ ὁ διαθέμενος.

'And for this end he is the mediator of the new
covenant, that, *his* death having taken place for the redemption of the transgressions under the first covenant,
they that are called might receive the promise of the
eternal inheritance.   For where a covenant *is*, there must
of necessity be brought in the death of the mediating
sacrifice.   For a covenant is valid over dead *sacrifices*:
since it is never of any force while the mediating *sacrifice*
continues alive.'

The death of the mediating sacrifice.] Here, as it seems
to me, lies the whole difficulty of the passage in its new
translation.   I feel not a shadow of difficulty about ἐπὶ
νεκροῖς, on which much has been written; nor about διαθέμενος being afterwards repeated in the masculine gender,
for I prefer taking διαθεμένου here as a masculine.   But
it is so clear that according to the legitimate use of διαθήκην διαθέσθαι, ὁ διαθέμενος is the party *who makes the covenant,* (as in chap. x. 16 of this Epistle, and in Aristoph.
Aves, 439—40: ἣν μὴ διαθῶνταί γ' οἵδε διαθήκην ἐμοὶ, Ἧπερ

ὁ πίθηκος τῇ γυναικὶ διέθετο,) that he must be a man of strong nerve who feels nothing of difficulty in giving it a different sense here. And though we are cautioned not to turn to Thucydides and Xenophon in order to understand the Greek of the New Testament, we must remember that the difference between them is to be found only in particular usages, and they are essentially the same language after all. We have a right therefore in this discussion to inquire, whether any other Greek writers have used the word διατίθεσθαι in the sense which is contended for in the new translation of this passage. And this inquiry must, I fear, be answered in the negative. The instance which Pierce brings from Appian, on the strength of which he translates ὁ διαθέμενος the pacifier, is to my mind by no means satisfactory: διαθέμενος τοὺς ἐνοχλοῦντας, *pacifying his troublesome creditors.* Nor do I think it of any use to the inquiry to adduce διατίθεσθαι ἔριν from Xenophon's Memorabilia.

Still, in the face of all this difficulty, I have proposed the above rendering, which, I believe, differs a little from all who have gone before me, though it agrees with many in its general principle. And, as in the case of words or phrases which are ἅπαξ λεγόμενα, we must make use of the context to assist us in eliciting the sense in which the writer meant his declaration to be understood. Let us, then, attend to the argument: *For this end,* viz. that he might purge our consciences from dead works to serve the living God, Jesus *is the mediator of the new covenant,* that BY HIS DEATH he might entitle us to the eternal inheritance. 'For (the strictness of his argument would require him to proceed) in a covenant THE MEDIATOR must die: else, how does the declaration of v. 16 assign a reason for that of v. 15? He became THE MEDIATOR of the covenant in order to answer the desired end; and this could not be without his death; for, that the covenant may be valid, there must be the death of the MEDIATOR, which can mean nothing but the MEDIATING SACRIFICE.—*In one sense,* perhaps, Moses was the mediator of the old covenant, and so a type of Christ; but *not in that sense* which required the death of the Mediator, which is clearly the sense required in v. 15, ἵνα θανάτου γενομένου, etc. In *that* sense the sacrifices, whose blood was sprinkled on the people (v. 19), were the types of Christ; and the point of coincidence between them as the types and Christ as the anti-type is, their being *mediating sacrifices* to ratify the respective covenants. Therefore the mediator expressed in διαθέμενος to answer to the μεσίτης must be the *mediating* SACRIFICE.

Now, upon the other view of the subject, the argument would clearly be inaccurate. 'Christ is the *Mediator* of the New Testament, that by his death he might procure us the blessings of the testament: FOR a testament requires the death of the *testator.*' Nay, he ought to have said, the death of the *Mediator.*——So that by that view we have a double confusion introduced into the Apostle's style: in the *general* argument we have *testament* and *covenant* confounded together; in the *particular* argument of this passage, we have the *testator* and the *mediator of the tes-*

tament confounded together:—if even any one can explain what *the mediator of a testament* is.

Over dead sacrifices] ἐπὶ νεκροῖς. Or it might be rendered, 'in the case of *its mediator* being put to death.' As the proposition is a general one, there is not the slightest objection to νεκροῖς being in the plural.—The construction of ἐπὶ νεκροῖς is the same as Eurip. Ion, v. 236: ἐπὶ δ' ἀσφάκτοις Μήλοισι δόμων μὴ πάριτ' εἰς μυχόν.

Since it is never of any force while] The simple declaration, *It is never of any force,* would require οὔποτε ἰσχύει, but the ἐπεὶ preceding will account for μὴ in place of οὔ. Others however would read it interrogatively, μή ποτε ἰσχύει, *does it ever avail?*

Ib. 23. *Should be purified.* καθαρίζεσθαι. 'Should be purged'—merely because the word is so translated in vv. 14, 22. also in chap. i. 3. x. 2, and other passages.

Ib. 24. *Into the holy places made with hands, which are the figures of the true.* εἰς χειροποίητα ἅγια . . . ἀντίτυπα τῶν ἀληθινῶν. 'Into the most holy *place* made with hands, *which is* a figure of the true.' And so again in v. 25 correct, 'into the most holy *place.*'

Ib. 28. *So Christ was once offered to bear the sins of many; and unto them that look for him shall he appear the second time without sin unto salvation.* οὕτως ὁ Χριστὸς ἅπαξ προσενεχθεὶς εἰς τὸ πολλῶν ἀνενεγκεῖν ἁμαρτίας, ἐκ δευτέρου χωρὶς ἁμαρτίας ὀφθήσεται τοῖς αὐτὸν ἀπεκδεχομένοις εἰς σωτηρίαν. 'So Christ, having been once offered to bear the sins of many, will appear the second time without sin unto salvation to them that look for him.' Breaking this

10

into two finite sentences interferes with the simplicity and compactness of the argument. The force of the comparison is—not, As it is appointed to men to die, so Christ died; but, As it is appointed to men to die once, and only once, and after that one death the judgment follows, so Christ, having fulfilled that law of our nature by dying once, will not die any more, but when he shall appear again, it will be not to die, but to bring salvation.

x. 17. *And their sins.* καὶ τῶν ἁμαρτιῶν αὐτῶν. 'Then he saith, And their sins*.' This, with only the difference of *said* for *saith*, is the reading of the margin: many Greek copies insert ὕστερον λέγει, or something to the same effect; and this reading has the sanction of the early versions. And it is absolutely necessary to the sense of the passage. The Apostle is insisting on the completeness of Christ's sacrifice in opposition to those of the law: the latter from their continual repetition made it evident that they did not *take away sin;* whereas Christ, *having offered one sacrifice for sins, perfected for ever them that were sanctified,* and

---

* May not an obscure passage in Psalm xci. 9, be cleared up by supplying the same verb which so many copies, from an obvious cause, omit in this verse? The authorised version is, "Because thou hast made the Lord, *which is* my refuge, *even* the Most High, thy habitation." This, it must be acknowledged, is awkward enough. The Prayer-book translation introduces confusion into the whole arrangement. The most literal rendering is, "Because thou, the Lord my refuge, hast made the Most High thy habitation." May it not be supplied from ver. 2, "Because thou *hast said,* The Lord *is* my refuge, *and* hast made the Most High thy habitation?" The verb *say* is similarly supplied by our Translators in Isaiah xli. 27.

procured a complete forgiveness, so that there was to be no further remembrance of their sins. And of this, he says, *the Holy Ghost is a witness*: for in Jeremiah's prophecy of the gospel-covenant, after all its other provisions and promises, he adds this, *Their sins and iniquities will I remember no more. Now where remission of these is, there is no more offering for sin.* This was the thing which the Holy Ghost's testimony was adduced to prove: complete and final forgiveness; consequently, no more sacrifice required. After enumerating therefore in the former part of the covenant all the other blessings, *then he saith, And their sins,* &c.

Ib. 27. *And fiery indignation.* καὶ πυρὸς ζῆλος. 'And a fiery indignation.' Otherwise the English is ambiguous, and sounds like *a looking for of fiery indignation.*

Ib. 38. *But if* any man *draw back.* καὶ ἐὰν ὑποστείλη- ται. 'But if he draw back.' Bishop Middleton on John viii. 44. seems to countenance the insertion of *any man* here by our Translators; but, without entering into any question about the doctrine involved in it, it seems to me unnecessary, and therefore I adhere to the letter of the original*.

---

* It should be observed, however, that some such insertion as that made by our Translators is countenanced by the *spirit* of the original, Habak. ii. 4, where the clause to which καὶ ἐὰν ὑπο- στείληται, &c. corresponds, comes in order before that in which *the just* is mentioned, and therefore *the just* cannot be the subject of it. In the Septuagint translation of the Prophet, which the Apostle quotes, ὑποστείληται can hardly be taken otherwise than with τις understood.

xi. 4. *By it he being dead yet speaketh.* δι᾽ αὐτῆς ἀποθα-
νὼν ἔτι λαλεῖται. 'Through it he being dead is yet spoken
of.' I adopt this rendering partly from the margin, understanding the reference of αὐτῆς to be to πίστει.

Ib. 7. *By the which.* δι᾽ ἧς. 'By which *faith.*' Without this insertion there is an ambiguity in the English.

Ib. 13. *And were persuaded* of them, &c. καὶ πει-
σθέντες. 'And being persuaded *of them,* and embracing
them, and confessing'—It is more simple to preserve the
participles to the end of the verse, than to change them
into verbs connected with *died.* The Apostle's object is
to state *how* they died.

xii. 9. *Unto the Father of spirits.* τῷ πατρὶ τῶν πνευμά-
των. 'To the Father of our spirits.' Opposed to τῆς
σαρκὸς ἡμῶν πατέρας. I do not mean that the common
translation is not equally *correct.*

Ib. 13. *Lest that which is lame be turned out of the
way ; but let it rather be healed.* ἵνα μὴ τὸ χωλὸν ἐκτραπῇ,
ἰαθῇ δὲ μᾶλλον. 'That the lame may not be turned
out of the way, but may rather be healed.' The latter
clause in the authorised version, *Let it be*—is quite inadmissible.

Ib. 17. *For ye know how that afterward, when he would
have inherited the blessing, he was rejected : for he found no
place of repentance, though he sought it carefully with tears.*
ἴστε γὰρ ὅτι καὶ μετέπειτα θέλων κληρονομῆσαι τὴν εὐλογίαν
ἀπεδοκιμάσθη· μετανοίας γὰρ τόπον οὐχ εὗρε, καίπερ μετὰ
δακρύων ἐκζητήσας αὐτήν. 'For ye know that even when
he afterwards desired to inherit the blessing, he was

rejected; for though he sought after it with tears, he found no room for repentance'—that is, as I understand it, no room or opportunity for his repentance to be availing. But the principal change made in the passage is the transposition of the two latter clauses; and the object of it is to mark the relation of the pronoun *it* (αὐτὴν) to *blessing* (εὐλογίαν). It cannot refer to *place* (τόπον), to which a mere English reader would naturally refer it; and between the two, εὐλογίαν and μετανοίας, it seems more simple, as well as more accordant with the historical fact (Gen. xxvii. 38), to connect it with the former.

Ib. 18.   *Unto the mount that might be touched.*   ψηλαφωμένῳ ὄρει. 'Unto the mount that could be touched.' The other is ambiguous, and *may be* mistaken to signify *the mount which it was* LAWFUL *to touch*—in direct opposition to the truth.   I remember hearing it remarked by an honest man, not deeply read in the original languages of Scripture, that "the reading here was no doubt a mistake—it ought to be *the mount that might* NOT *be touched!*"

xiii. 4.   *Marriage* is *honourable in all, and the bed undefiled.* τίμιος ὁ γάμος ἐν πᾶσι, καὶ ἡ κοίτη ἀμίαντος. '*Let* marriage *be* honoured with all, and the bed *be* undefiled.' Otherwise the latter clause will make a difficulty on account of the Article being before κοίτη, which will prevent κοίτη and ἀμίαντος being in immediate concord.   The order and construction are thus precisely the same as in the next verse, ἀφιλάργυρος ὁ τρόπος.—I marvel that the Rhemish Translators did not hit upon the right rendering

here, to make the best use they could of it in favour
of celibacy: but their version is *singularly faithful, Marriage honourable in all, and the bed undefiled.*—I beg their
pardon: I have since observed, that they have in a note
corrected as I have done, and added some remarks,
grounded on St Paul's example, against the *compulsory
obligation* of marriage.

Ib. 8. *Jesus Christ, the same yesterday, and to-day, and
for ever.* Ἰησοῦς Χριστὸς χθὲς καὶ σήμερον ὁ αὐτὸς, καὶ εἰς
τοὺς αἰῶνας. 'Jesus Christ *is* the same yesterday, and to-
day, and for ever.' From the peculiarity of the common
version many persons are led to connect this verse with
the preceding: and indeed some editions compel them to
this course by placing only a colon at the end of the preceding verse; though very improperly, as the early editions
uniformly, I believe, have the period there. But the order
of the words in the Greek of v. 7, as well as the train of
thought, seems decidedly opposed to such a connexion*.
—Supplying a verb to the sentence as I have done above,
I connect the verse with the following: *Jesus Christ is the
same;* therefore be ye the same, and *be not carried about
with divers and strange doctrines,* but let *the heart be established;* in order to which establishment, seek for more
grace, and do not go back to *meats* and other observances
of the Mosaic ritual, *which have not profited them that have*

---

* The late Rev. Robert Hall closes his celebrated "Character"
of Mr Robinson with a quotation of ver. 7, in a new translation
which happily removes all ambiguity: *And, considering the end of
their conversation, imitate their faith.*

been occupied therein. And besides, this mixing up of the law will shut you out from the gospel; for *we have an altar,* &c.

Ib. 15. *The fruit of our lips, giving thanks to his name.* καρπὸν χειλέων ὁμολογούντων τῷ ὀνόματι αὐτοῦ. 'The fruit of lips giving thanks to his name.' From the received translation and punctuation it would not have been suspected that *giving* was in concord with *lips.*

THE EPISTLE OF ST JAMES.

CHAP. ii. 2. *In goodly apparel.* ἐν ἐσθῆτι λαμπρᾷ. 'In gay clothing,' as the words are translated in the next verse; and there is no imaginable reason for any variation. Of the two renderings, that which I have preferred better represents the original. In Acts x. 30. the same words are rendered *in bright clothing.*

Ib. 14. *Can faith save him?* μὴ δύναται ἡ πίστις σῶσαι αὐτόν; 'Can his faith save him?'—such a faith as he professes to have? The Article, which is omitted in our translation, clearly marks the reference to the πίστιν preceding.

Ib. 21. *When he had offered.* ἀνενέγκας. 'In offering.' Same tense with ἐδικαιώθη. See on Luke xxiii. 46. The argument has some difficulty in itself; and there is no need to add to the inherent perplexity by affixing to this action a time so definitely marked. Strictly speaking,

Abraham had been justified long before: and all that this
action did towards it was the evidence it supplied of the
nature of the faith by which he was justified. It was a
working faith. A remark nearly similar may be applied to
the translation of ὑποδεξαμένη, v. 25.

iii. 3. *We put bits in the horses' mouths.* τῶν ἵππων
τοὺς χαλινοὺς εἰς τὰ στόματα βάλλομεν. 'We put the
horses' bits into their mouths'—intimating the seat of
the mischiefs he is here deprecating, those of the *tongue,*
and to which therefore the remedy must be applied. For,
as he had in effect said in the preceding verse, if a man
can bridle his tongue, he is *able to bridle the whole body.*

Ib. 9. *God, even the Father.* τὸν Θεὸν καὶ πατέρα.
'Our God and Father.' The other would restrict it to
the first Person of the Godhead. For καὶ, *even,* see on
Coloss. ii. 2.—But on the whole question see the note on
1 Corinth. xv. 24.

Ib. 14. *Glory not, and lie not against the truth.* μὴ
κατακαυχᾶσθε καὶ ψεύδεσθε κατὰ τῆς ἀληθείας. 'Do not glory
and lie against the truth.' The latter words are dependent
on both the verbs.

iv. 5. *Do ye think that the scripture saith in vain,*
The spirit that dwelleth in us lusteth to envy? ἢ δοκεῖτε ὅτι
κενῶς ἡ γραφὴ λέγει; πρὸς φθόνον ἐπιποθεῖ τὸ πνεῦμα ὃ κατῴ-
κησεν ἐν ἡμῖν; 'Do ye think that the scripture speaketh
vainly? Doth the Spirit that dwelleth in us lust to
envy?'—To the authorised translation there are serious
objections. The passage which it represents as a quotation from scripture, is no where to be found there, nor

any thing sufficiently near to it to pass for another form of what the Apostle had in his mind. Nor, if it were so, would it make any thing of a clear argument in connexion with the context. Nor finally, if we take πνεῦμα in the sense of the *human disposition*, as seems in this view to be necessary, does it appear capable of explanation why this should be called *the spirit that dwelleth in us*, which on the other hand is a very usual and proper and intelligible description of the Holy Spirit, who comes into believers for the very purpose. Compare Romans viii. 11. and 2 Tim. i. 14.—The other method of arranging and understanding the passage before us is now supported by so many commentators, that nothing need be added to recommend it, except a word or two as to its connexion. The former clause stands connected with a declaration, that *the friendship of the world is enmity with God;* and therefore must be understood to mean, *Do ye think that* the declarations of *scripture* on this subject are *in vain?* The latter clause, according to the common interpretation, is more difficult; because the Apostle is not cautioning against *envy*, but *worldliness;* whereas they make it import, Is not this envious spirit contrary to the Spirit of God that dwelleth in us? The marginal rendering of πρὸς φθόνον is *enviously;* and I would suggest for consideration, whether ἐπιποθεῖ πρὸς φθόνον, *lusteth enviously* or *grudgingly*, may not signify, *to be of a grudging disposition*, (compare chap. i. 5;) and so the import of the whole be, Seeing it is so necessary to mortify this love of the world, seek for the Holy Spirit's help to enable you to do it ; and do not think that his grace will be withheld; for *is he grudgingly affected?* Nay, *but he giveth more grace.*—But whatever be thought of the interpretation, the translation certainly needs correction.

v. 17. *On the earth.* ἐπὶ τῆς γῆς. 'On the land.' See on Luke xxiii. 44.

Ib. 20. *The sinner.* ἁμαρτωλόν. 'A sinner.' The proposition is general. So free, unhappily, did our Translators make with the Article, that they scrupled not at either its insertion or omission: the latter is much more frequent with them.

THE FIRST EPISTLE OF ST PETER.

CHAP. i. 3. *Blessed* be *the God and Father of our Lord Jesus Christ.* εὐλογητὸς ὁ Θεὸς καὶ πατὴρ τοῦ Κυρίου ἡμῶν Ἰησοῦ Χριστοῦ. 'Blessed *be* God the Father of our Lord Jesus Christ.' For the sense of the phrase ὁ Θεὸς καὶ πατὴρ, see on 1 Corinth. xv. 24—and if the conclusion there be correct, that ὁ Θεὸς καὶ πατὴρ designates him who is God and the Father, and is properly expressed by *God the Father;* the translation of these words will not be affected by the circumstance of πατὴρ being followed by a genitive expressing the object of the relation. There seems no reason in such a case for understanding this genitive as dependent on both the preceding nominatives. In Romans xv. 6, τὸν Θεὸν καὶ πατέρα τοῦ Κυρίου ἡμῶν Ἰησοῦ Χριστοῦ is rendered, *God, even the Father of our Lord Jesus Christ.*

This translation should be corrected as in the passage before us.

Ib. 7. *At the appearing of Jesus Christ.* ἐν ἀποκαλύψει Ἰησοῦ Χριστοῦ. 'At the revelation of Jesus Christ.' So the words are rendered, more accurately, in v. 13.

Ib. 11. *Searching what or what manner of time the Spirit of Christ which was in them did signify, when it testified beforehand the sufferings of Christ.* ἐρευνῶντες εἰς τίνα ἢ ποῖον καιρὸν ἐδήλου τὸ ἐν αὐτοῖς πνεῦμα Χριστοῦ προμαρτυρόμενον τὰ εἰς Χριστὸν παθήματα. 'Searching in regard to what or what manner of time the Spirit of Christ in them did shew and testify beforehand the sufferings of Christ:' or, 'the Spirit of Christ which prophesied in them signified the sufferings of Christ.' Compare Acts xxviii. 23, οἷς ἐξετίθετο διαμαρτυρόμενος τὴν βασιλείαν τοῦ Θεοῦ. The authorised version cannot be right in making καιρὸν the object after ἐδήλου, and passing over the preposition εἰς.

ii. 4. *But chosen of God, and precious.* παρὰ δὲ Θεῷ ἐκλεκτὸν, ἔντιμον. 'But in God's sight elect *and* precious.' The other translation restricts παρὰ Θεῷ to one of the adjectives, when it clearly belongs to both, as implied in the quotation, v. 6.

Ib. 7. *He is precious,* marg. *an honour.* ἡ τιμή. 'The preciousness *belongs*,' i. e. the preciousness which is in Christ, as declared in the preceding verses.

Ib. 13. *Submit yourselves.* ὑποτάγητε οὖν. 'Submit yourselves therefore.' It is remarkable that so important a word as οὖν, marking the connexion with the preceding verse, should have been omitted by our Translators. It is however wanting in some MSS.

iii. 13. *If ye be followers of that which is good.* ἐὰν τοῦ ἀγαθοῦ μιμηταὶ γένησθε. 'If ye be followers of him who is good.' μιμηταὶ is *followers of an example*, not of *an object; imitators.* Compare Ephes. v. 1 and Matt. xix. 17. I ought not however to withhold another passage, 3 Epist. John, 11; but there τὸ κακὸν and τὸ ἀγαθὸν have an immediate reference to the examples adduced in the preceding and following verses.

Ib. 14. *And be not afraid of their terror.* τὸν δὲ φόβον αὐτῶν μὴ φοβηθῆτε. 'And fear not their fear.' So the Hebrew is properly translated in Isai. viii. 12, as the sense requires: when they cry out in terror, 'A confederacy' (see Isai. vii. 2), be not ye terrified like them; but sanctify, &c.

Ib. 20. *Were saved by water.* διεσώθησαν δι' ὕδατος. 'Were saved through the water;' i. e. not by means of, but were preserved through it, during its continuance, and brought safe out of it. So in 1 Timoth. ii. 15, where however the authorised translation, *in child-bearing,* expresses with sufficient accuracy the force of διά. So Xenophon, Anab. v. 5, 7, διὰ πολλῶν τε καὶ δεινῶν πραγμάτων σεσωμένοι πάρεστε. Compare 1 Corinth. iii. 15, and the note there.

iv. 8. *Shall cover the multitude of sins.* καλύψει πλῆθος ἁμαρτιῶν. 'Will cover a multitude of sins.' In what sense, will appear from Proverbs x. 12, of which it is a quotation.

v. 13. *And* so doth *Marcus my son.* καὶ Μάρκος ὁ

υἱός μου. 'And Mark my son.' As this form of the name is preserved in other passages, it is desirable to retain it here for the purpose of marking the identity.

THE SECOND EPISTLE OF ST PETER.

CHAP. i. 1. *To them that have obtained like precious faith with us through the righteousness of God and our Saviour Jesus Christ.* τοῖς ἰσότιμον ἡμῖν λαχοῦσι πίστιν ἐν δικαιοσύνῃ τοῦ Θεοῦ ἡμῶν καὶ σωτῆρος Ἰησοῦ Χριστοῦ. 'To them that have obtained like precious faith with us in the righteousness of our God and Saviour Jesus Christ.'

Faith in the righteousness] In it, as the object of faith, as in Romans iii. 25, διὰ τῆς πίστεως ἐν τῷ αὐτοῦ αἵματι. Eph. i. 15, τὴν καθ᾽ ὑμᾶς πίστιν ἐν τῷ Κυρίῳ Ἰησοῦ. So also Galat. iii. 26. I hardly see what definite meaning is to be attached to the common translation, *through the righteousness.*

Of our God and Saviour] The same construction as in v. 11, *Of our Lord and Saviour Jesus Christ.* See on Ephes. v. 5. Titus ii. 13. The new translation here proposed is in fact inserted in the margin; but it is an insertion of recent date, and not made by the Translators.

Ib. 3. *That hath called us to glory and virtue.* τοῦ καλέσαντος ἡμᾶς διὰ δόξης καὶ ἀρετῆς. 'That hath called us by glory and power.' *By,* as in the margin: and so the *glory* will refer to the mission of the Son (compare John i. 14 and xi. 40), and the *power* to that of the Holy Ghost.

No imaginable latitude in the use of the prepositions can justify the common translation, *to glory.*

Ib. 4. *Whereby are given unto us.* δι' ὧν ἡμῖν δεδώρηται. 'Whereby he hath given unto us.' That it may be thus translated, no one will question: that it ought to be, I infer from a general inspection of the passage, and from the similar use of δεδωρημένης in the preceding verse.

Ib. ib. *Having escaped the corruption.* ἀποφυγόντες τῆς ... φθορᾶς. 'Having escaped from the corruption.' Not, having escaped its entanglement, but, having escaped from it after being entangled.

Ib. 5. *And besides this.* καὶ αὐτὸ τοῦτο δέ. 'And for this very reason.' I consider it quite certain, that neither the Greek words nor the sense of the passage will admit of the common rendering. The words are used in a very similar manner in Eurip. Orest. 657—8: ἐρεῖς, ἀδύνατον; αὐτὸ τοῦτο, τοὺς φίλους 'Εν τοῖς κακοῖς χρὴ τοῖς φίλοισιν ὠφελεῖν. The ellipses may in both cases be supplied by κατὰ or διά. Thucyd. v. 106, ἡμεῖς δὲ κατ' αὐτὸ τοῦτο ἤδη καὶ μάλιστα πιστεύομεν. In 2 Corinth. ii. 3, καὶ ἔγραψα ὑμῖν τοῦτο αὐτό, ἵνα μὴ—it is doubtful whether τοῦτο αὐτὸ be the object after the verb, or be not rather used as in the present passage, *for this very purpose.*

Ib. 16. *For we have not followed cunningly devised fables, when we made known unto you.* οὐ γὰρ σεσοφισμένοις μύθοις ἐξακολουθήσαντες ἐγνωρίσαμεν ὑμῖν. 'For we did not follow cunningly-devised fables, when we made known unto you.' A double confusion of tenses is introduced by our Translators in this verse by their fondness for the form of the preter-perfect: *we have not followed* can hardly agree either with *we made known* or *were eye-witnesses.*—But the whole verse may be better and more correctly translated: *For* it was *not from having followed cunningly devised fables* that *we made known to you the power and coming of our Lord Jesus Christ, but from having been eye-witnesses of his majesty.*

Ib. 18. *And this voice which came from heaven we heard.* καὶ ταύτην τὴν φωνὴν ἡμεῖς ἠκούσαμεν ἐξ οὐρανοῦ ἐνεχθεῖσαν. 'And this voice we heard come from heaven.' Our Translators have rendered it as if it were τὴν ἐνεχθεῖσαν, to the manifest injury of the sense.

ii. 5. *Noah the eighth* person. ὄγδοον Νῶε. 'Noah with seven others,' according to the well-known sense of this form of speech.

Ib. 14. *Cursed children.* κατάρας τέκνα. 'Children of the curse,' or 'of cursing.' This is not one of those common Hebraisms which abound in the writings of the Apostles, in which a quality of the subject is expressed by a genitive following it, instead of an adjective in concord with it; such as Luke xvi. 8, *the steward of injustice* for *the unjust steward.* Even in these I think our venerable Translators would sometimes have done better by retaining the simplicity of the original form, as in Coloss. i. 13, *the Son of his love* instead of *his dear Son.* But at all events in the passage now before us it is to be observed, that the persons do not bear the character of *children* at all except in relation to the *curse* with which that word is connected; and therefore if the phrase was to be divested of this form, it ought to have been rendered *cursed persons*, the relation of *children* being implied in the connexion in which they are thus placed with *the curse*. They have done better therefore in Ephes. ii. 2, in preserving the form, *children of disobedience*.

Ib. 18. *When they speak.* φθεγγόμενοι. 'By speaking.'

iii. 12. *Hasting unto.* σπεύδοντας. 'Hastening on.' Parkhurst aptly quotes Thucyd. vi. 39, fin. κακὰ σπεύδοντες, though his translation of the word is unnecessarily remote from the original, *desiring earnestly*. Of the literal translation, *hastening on*, though of course it is not to be taken in its literal sense, a good illustration is in Judges v. 28: "The mother of Sisera looked out at a window, and cried through the lattice, Why is his chariot *so* long in coming? why tarry the wheels of his chariots?"

Ib. 16. *In which are some things.* ἐν οἷς ἐστί τινα. 'In which things are some *matters*.' Without the insertion of *things* the obvious reference of *which* would be to *epistles*.

THE FIRST EPISTLE OF ST JOHN.

CHAP. v. 15. *And if we know that he hear us.* καὶ ἐὰν οἴδαμεν ὅτι ἀκούει ἡμῶν. 'And if we know that he heareth us.' This singular mistake pervades, I believe, all the editions of the authorised translation.

Ib. 16. *He shall give him life for them that sin not unto*

death. δώσει αὐτῷ ζωὴν, τοῖς ἁμαρτάνουσι μὴ πρὸς θάνατον. 'He shall give him life, *even* to them that sin not unto death.' I suppose that the construction δίδωμι σοι ἐκείνῳ, *I give to you for him,* is altogether without a precedent in any Greek author whatever*; and there is no possible reason for fabricating such a construction here. The reference of αὐτῷ is evidently to the ἀδελφὸς that has sinned, not to him that prays for him; and the τοῖς ἁμαρτάνουσι, etc. is an epexegesis, by which the Apostle both limits and enlarges the promise, so as to include those only who sin not unto death, but all of that class.

Ib. ib. *I do not say that he shall pray for it.* οὐ περὶ ἐκείνης λέγω ἵνα ἐρωτήσῃ. 'For that I do not say that he shall pray.' The common translation loses sight of the marked emphasis expressed by ἐκείνης.

Ib. 19. *In wickedness.* ἐν τῷ πονηρῷ. 'In the wicked one;' a strong expression to signify *under his influence.*

THE THIRD EPISTLE OF ST JOHN.

VER. 10. *I will remember.* ὑπομνήσω. 'I will bring to remembrance.'

---

* Aristoph. Vesp. 678—9, will hardly be considered a case in point: σοὶ δ' * * * οὐδεὶς οὐδὲ σκορόδου κεφαλὴν τοῖς ἑψητοῖσι δίδωσι.

THE GENERAL EPISTLE OF ST JUDE.

VER. 3. *When I gave all diligence to write unto you of the common salvation, it was needful for me to write unto you, and exhort* you. πᾶσαν σπουδὴν ποιούμενος γράφειν ὑμῖν περὶ τῆς κοινῆς σωτηρίας, ἀνάγκην ἔσχον γράψαι ὑμῖν παρακαλῶν. 'Being earnestly desirous to write unto you of the common salvation, I am compelled to write to exhort you.' The ὑμῖν being dependent on γράψαι, it would be necessary to supply ὑμᾶς after παρακαλῶν, which would needlessly encumber the sentence: the sense is made clear by transferring the personal case after the participle. The past tense of ἀνάγκην ἔσχον γράψαι seems to me to be only another form of the well-known usage of ἔγραψα where *our* idiom would lead us to expect γράφω; and the connexion of the whole is very clear: My wish was to write to you *of the common salvation,* and the general doctrines of the gospel; but I am obliged to use a particular topic of exhortation, from the circumstance of *certain men having crept in unawares* (rather, *insidiously, craftily,*) &c.

4. *And denying the only Lord God, and our Lord Jesus Christ.* καὶ τὸν μόνον δεσπότην Θεὸν καὶ Κύριον ἡμῶν, Ἰησοῦν Χριστὸν ἀρνούμενοι. 'And denying the only master our God and Lord Jesus Christ.' Assuming the correctness of the above reading of the original, I propose this amendment of the translation; and in the corresponding passage, 2 Peter ii. 1, I would render, *denying the master*

that bought them. It is obviously very awkward and anomalous, in such a passage as the present, to translate δεσπότην and Κύριον by the same English word *Lord.* In the Geneva version δεσπότην is rendered *master,* in the Rhemish *dominator.* There is also a variety in the modes of arranging the construction of the words; Tyndale, Cranmer, and the Geneva version taking it, *denying God the only Lord, and our Lord Jesus Christ.* It is difficult to reconcile this with the fact of there being only one article prefixed to all the words: we should expect καὶ TON Κύριον.

But in the original text many MSS. and versions omit Θεόν· it is of course wanting also in 2 Pet. ii. 1: and doubtless the omission of the word makes the whole flow more smoothly. But as St Peter there defines the δεσπό-της referred to by annexing the exegetical words τὸν ἀγοράσαντα αὐτούς, so St Jude, writing after him, might doubtless see occasion to vary his speech, not only by specifying the person intended, but by marking his divine dignity in opposition to those who probably denied it, while they rejected his service.

8. *Likewise also these.* ὁμοίως μέντοι καὶ οὗτοι. 'In like manner nevertheless these also.' Nevertheless, i. e. notwithstanding the terrible example of v. 7.

THE REVELATION OF ST JOHN.

CHAP. ii. 22. *Behold, I will cast her into a bed, and them that commit adultery with her into great tribulation.* ἰδοὺ ἐγὼ βάλλω αὐτὴν εἰς κλίνην, καὶ τοὺς μοιχεύοντας μετ᾽ αὐτῆς, εἰς θλίψιν μεγάλην. 'Behold, I will cast her into a bed, and *her* adulterers with her, *even* into great tribulation.' Most editions print it without the comma at αὐτῆς. So μετ᾽ αὐτῆς is connected with μοιχεύοντας, and the punishment of Jezebel is separated from that of her adulterers: besides which *casting her into a bed* is much too indefinite to suit the scope of the passage. I prefer to make μετ᾽ αὐτῆς dependent on βάλλω, giving to the article τοὺς its possessive force, and consider the θλίψιν μεγάλην as exegetical of κλίνην, according to the common usage of the prophetic style, to clothe an idea first in figurative language, and then exhibit it naked without a figure: *I will cast them into a bed* together; not a bed of lust, but of *great tribulation*.—If it be preferred to preserve the connexion of μετ᾽ αὐτῆς with μοιχεύοντας, (and certainly the view I have taken would be more properly expressed by σὺν αὐτῇ,) the other correction must still be recommended: *I will cast her and those who commit adultery with her into a bed*, even *into great tribulation*.

Ib. 27. *As the vessels of a potter shall they be broken to shivers.* ὡς τὰ σκεύη τὰ κεραμικὰ συντρίβεται. 'As the vessels of a potter are broken in pieces.' The authorised version is a translation of a different reading in the Greek text, συντριβήσεται, which Griesbach marks as of nearly equal authority with the other, but to which there are very serious objections. The matter also is made worse by Griesbach and others by putting a colon instead of a comma at σιδηρᾷ, and thus almost necessitating the adoption of the wrong construction. In this arrangement the subject of συντριβήσεται is αὐτοὶ understood from αὐτοὺς in the preceding clause; a construction which in a different form is very rarely met with in the poets, but which of course is utterly inadmissible in the present case. Besides which, a strange incongruity is introduced between this and the following clause: *they shall be broken, as I have received.* In the other construction all is in harmony: *he shall rule them* (ποιμανεῖ, the Sept. translation of Psal. ii. 9, תְּרֹעֵם *thou shalt break them*), and thus exercise the power which *I have received of my Father.* For a striking illustration of the figure see Jerem. xix. 1—11.

iii. 8. *And no man can shut it.* καὶ οὐδεὶς δύναται κλεῖσαι αὐτήν. 'And none can shut it.' See on John x. 29.

iv. 4. *And round about the throne* were *four and twenty seats.* καὶ κυκλόθεν τοῦ θρόνου θρόνοι εἴκοσι καὶ τέσσαρες. 'And round about the throne *were* four and twenty thrones.' The same word is repeated in the original with such evident intention, as appears from the juxta-position θρόνου θρόνοι, that we lose something of the character of the passage by a change. And there is clearly no danger of *the throne* of God being confounded with *the thrones* of the four and twenty elders.—Several other passages in the following chapters of this book, where these thrones of the elders are spoken of, require the same correction.

Ib. 6. *Four beasts.* τέσσαρα ζῶα. 'Four living creatures.' The propriety of this correction is now, I believe, generally agreed upon by commentators. The word is very different from θηρίον, used to designate the prophetic Beast in the 13th and following chapters.

v. 3. *And no man.* καὶ οὐδείς. 'And no one.' See on chap. iii. 8.

vii. 14. *Out of great tribulation.* ἐκ τῆς θλίψεως τῆς μεγάλης 'Out of the great tribulation.' The Articles would hardly have been inserted, if it had not been intended to mark something specific,—*the great tribulation* of the ten celebrated persecutions.

x. 6. *That there should be time no longer.* ὅτι χρόνος οὐκ ἔσται ἔτι. 'That there should be no more delay.' I do not see how either the common translation, or another which has been proposed, *that the time should not be yet,* can give a satisfactory sense. Perhaps indeed our Translators intended to convey by their version the same sense which is more clearly expressed by the word *delay,* using *time* for *time intervening.* The scope of the passage is, that without any further delay, upon the sounding of the seventh angel, *the mystery of God should be finished.*

xi. 3. *And I will give* power *unto my two witnesses, and they shall prophesy.* καὶ δώσω τοῖς δυσὶ μάρτυσί μου, καὶ προφητεύσουσιν. 'And I will give unto my two witnesses that they may prophesy'—according to a common use of the Hebrew).

Ib. 19. *The ark of his testament.* ἡ κιβωτὸς τῆς δια-θήκης αὐτοῦ. 'The ark of his covenant.' See on Hebrews ix. 15.

xiii. 16. *To receive.* Margin, *Gr. to give.* ἵνα δώσῃ αὐτοῖς. The marginal reading is decidedly wrong with the *appearance* of correctness, and that of the text entirely accurate and even elegant. The literal arrangement of the original, vv. 16—7, is, *And he causeth all—that he should give to them—and that no man might buy—*The received translation therefore conveys the spirit of the original, and sufficiently satisfies the letter*.

xiv. 3. *And no man could learn that song.* καὶ οὐδεὶς ἠδύνατο μαθεῖν τὴν ᾠδήν. 'And no one could learn the song.' See on John x. 29.

xv. 2. *Stand on the sea of glass.* ἑστῶτας ἐπὶ τὴν θάλασ-σαν τὴν ὑαλίνην. 'Stand by the sea of glass;' as in John iv. 6, *on the well,* ἐπὶ τῇ πηγῇ, *at the well.* The difference of case is not important in the writings of St John.

xvi. 10. *The seat of the beast.* τὸν θρόνον τοῦ θηρίου. 'The throne of the beast.' Similarly in xiii. 2.

xvii. 10. *And there are seven kings.* καὶ βασιλεῖς ἑπτά εἰσιν. 'And they are seven kings.' It might be, 'And they are *also* seven kings.' It is clearly the design of the passage to express, that the *seven heads*, which represented *seven mountains,* represented also seven forms of government. The common translation merely predicates the existence of *seven kings.*

---

* The above note assumes the correctness of the received reading, δώσῃ. But Griesbach admits into the text δῶσιν, and other copies have δώσουσιν, δώσωσιν.

xviii. 13. *And sheep, and horses, and chariots, and slaves, and souls of men.* καὶ πρόβατα, καὶ ἵππων, καὶ ῥεδῶν, καὶ σωμάτων, καὶ ψυχὰς ἀνθρώπων. 'And sheep, and *the merchandise* of horses, and of chariots, and of slaves, and souls of men.' The transition from the accusative to the genitive; after the genitive had been used in the beginning of the sentence, is so remarkable that there must be some reason for it, and it ought to be expressed in a translation. I understand γόμον from γόμον χρυσοῦ in the preceding verse.

xix. 16. *A name written.* τὸ ὄνομα γεγραμμένον. 'His name written.'

xx. 4. *And which had not worshipped.* καὶ οἵτινες οὐ προσεκύνησαν. 'And whosoever worshipped not.' Compare ii. 24.

xxi. 12. *And had a wall.* ἔχουσάν τε τεῖχος. 'And it had a wall.' It is as well to relinquish the participial form, on account of what has intervened since the former ἔχουσαν, with which it is connected; but then the verb introduced must be supplied with a nominative case.

xxii. 2. Was there *the tree of life.* ξύλον ζωῆς. '*Was a tree of life.*' This is Bishop Middleton's correction, in order to avoid the inconsistency of saying, that *the* ONE *tree* was on each side of the river. Another interpretation, however, has been advanced by Dr Owen, which is entitled to some consideration: 'And the river *being* on either side *of it.*' And this might be carried even a little farther: "In the midst of the street of it and of the river, *being* (viz. both *the street* and *the river* being) on either side of it," (the tree.)

EXCURSUS

On Luke XI. 28.

Μενοῦνγε. *Yea, rather.* No remark is necessary on this passage with a view to *correcting* the translation, which seems to be sufficiently accurate; and therefore I have passed over it in the preceding pages : but in the phrase thus translated there is peculiarity enough to make it worth a brief investigation, in regard to its use both in sacred and profane writers. The passages in which μὲν οὖν without γε are combined in their ordinary sense, as Luke iii. 18, πολλὰ μὲν οὖν, κ. τ. λ. will not require notice. Philippians iii. 8, ἀλλὰ μενοῦνγε, *Yea doubtless,* may also be passed over, as the insertion of ἀλλὰ gives a different character to the expression.

There remain two, and I believe only two, passages in the New Testament, where the particles occur compounded as in the present passage. Romans ix. 19, 20: Ἐρεῖς οὖν μοι, Τί ἔτι μέμφεται; τῷ γὰρ βουλήματι αὐτοῦ τίς ἀνθέστηκε; Μενοῦνγε, ὦ ἄνθρωπε, σὺ τίς εἶ—*Nay but, O man.* Again, x. 18, Ἀλλὰ λέγω, Μὴ οὐκ ἤκουσαν; μενοῦνγε εἰς πᾶσαν τὴν γῆν— *Yes verily.* Turning to profane authors, the passages in which the usage seems to come nearest to that of the Greek Testament are Aristoph. Acharn. 272, 3: τὴν χύτραν συντρίψετε. Σὲ μὲν οὖν—(*Nay, rather you.*) Vesp. 953, where γε is added, κλέπτης μὲν οὖν οὗτός γε. Equit. 908: ἐμοῦ μὲν οὖν, ἐμοῦ μὲν οὖν. *No, mine.* A passage in Euripides, Phœniss. 561, is also worth attention, where κενὸν μὲν οὖν occurs in answer to a question. In the Agamemnon of Æschylus, 1367, ὑπερδίκως μὲν οὖν, if the punctuation which Wellauer prefers be adopted, (though he is too positive and over-bearing in maintaining it,) the sense will be, *Nay, supremely just.*

Comparing these passages with those from the Greek Testament, two points of difference appear between them, that in the profane writers μὲν οὖν does not begin the sentence, and that it is not followed by γε, except in one instance, and then not immediately. The decision of Viger, viii. 8. 15, is, that it cannot stand at the beginning of a sentence, except when γε follows; which appears to be correct, for the example quoted by Wetstein from Aristotle Poet. § 22, μὲν οὖν φαίνεσθαι is in all the good copies τὸ μὲν οὖν. And even with the γε there is no classical authority for so placing it; but μενοῦγγε must be considered an usage peculiar to the New Testament—so far at least as classical writers are concerned. Schleusner's interpretation of it is accurate: "Est particula fortiter negandi et contrarium affirmandi." To which it may be added, by way of explanation, that when it follows an affirmative proposition, it expresses a negative; and when a negative, the contrary. On this principle, the passage of St Luke would be rendered with more strict accuracy, NAY *rather*—but indeed the word *rather* implies the negation.   And in Aristoph. Acharn. 273, which my learned friend, Mr Mitchell, explains *Nay, yea rather,* it is not quite an indifferent matter, but the former rendering would be a little more exact.

ADDENDUM.

1 Corinth. x. 17.   Compare with this passage Romans xii. 5.

1. INDEX OF AUTHORS CITED.

2. GENERAL INDEX.

By Professor Scholefield.

Lately Published.

1. Baptismal Regeneration as maintained by the Church of England. A Sermon before the University. *Third Edition.* Price 1s.

2. The Christian Altar. A Sermon before the University. *Second Edition,* with an Appendix. Price 1s. 6d.

3. Scriptural Grounds of Union. Five Sermons before the University. *Second Edition.* Price 3s. 6d.

4. An Argument for a Church Establishment. A Sermon before the University. *Second Edition.* Price 1s.

5. The Golden Pipes: The Word of the Lord to England. A Sermon preached at the Consecration of Emmanuel Church, Weston super Mare. Price 1s.

EDUCATIONAL BOOKS.

PUBLISHED BY

JOHN W. PARKER AND SON, WEST STRAND.

Outlines of the History of England. Cheaper Edition. 1s.

Outlines of the History of Ireland. By O. COCKAYNE, M.A., one of the Classical Masters, King's College School. 1s.

Outlines of the History of France. By O. COCKAYNE, M.A. 1s. 3d.

Outlines of Roman History. With Wood-cuts, &c. 10d.

Outlines of Grecian History. By the Rev. B. BOUCHIER, M.A. With Maps and Views. 1s.

Outlines of Sacred History. Cheaper Edition. 2s. 6d.

Outlines of Ecclesiastical History. By Rev. W. H. HOARE, M.A., late Fellow of St. John's College, Cambridge. 2s. 6d.

Bible Narrative chronologically arranged. With Maps. 7s.

Elements of Ancient History. With Questions. 2s.

Elements of Modern History. With Questions. 2s

School History of England, abridged from Gleig's Family History; with Chronology, List of Contemporary Sovereigns, and Questions. 6s.
'The best of the numerous class especially written for instruction.'—
Quarterly Review.

Heads of an Analysis of English History, and of French History. By DAWSON W. TURNER, M.A., Head Master of the Royal Institution, Liverpool. 2s.

Heads of an Analysis of Roman History. By the same. 2s.

First Ideas of Geography for Beginners. 1s.

Outlines of Geography. With Maps and Woodcuts. 10d.

Descriptive Geography, a Familiar Account of the various Countries of the World. With Popular Statistics. 2s.

Outlines of Geology. By Miss R. M. ZORNLIN. With Illustrations. 10d.

Outlines of Physical Geography. By Miss R. M. ZORNLIN. With Maps. 10d.

Recreations in Physical Geography. By the same Author. With Woodcuts and Plates. 6s.

Guyot's Earth and Man; or, Physical Geography in its relation to the History of Mankind. Slightly abridged, with corrections and notes. 2s. 6d.

Manual of Ancient Geography; with the Names of Places marked with their proper Quantities. By W. HILDYARD, M.A. 2s. 6d.

Hand-Book of Bible Geography. A brief alphabetical description of the ancient and modern condition of the chief places mentioned in the Bible. 2s.

Bible Maps for Schools; with brief descriptions. Sewed, 3s.

Bible Maps; an Historical and Descriptive Atlas. With copious Index. By W. HUGHES, F.R.G.S. 7s. 6d. coloured.

Outline Scripture-Maps: By J. R. MAJOR, M.A., one of the Classical Masters in King's College, London. With the Key, 3s.

Manual of Geographical Science. The First Part containing Mathematical Geography, by M. O'BRIEN, M.A., Professor of Natural Philosophy in King's College. Physical Geography, by D. T. ANSTED, M.A., F.R.S., Professor of Geology in King's College. Chartography, by J. R. JACKSON, F.R.S., late Secretary of the Royal Geographical Society. Terminology and Theory of Description, by the Rev. C. G. NICOLAY, Librarian of King's College. 8vo. 10s. 6d.

Atlas of Physical and Historical Geography. Engraved by J. W. LOWRY. Under the direction of PROFESSOR ANSTED and the Rev. C. G. NICOLAY, F.R.G.S. 5s.

Outlines of Chemistry. By T. GRIFFITHS. 10*d*.

Outlines of Astronomy. By Professor HALL, of King's
College. 10*d*.

Elements of Algebra. By Professor HALL, of King's
College. Cheaper Edition. 5*s*.

Figures of Euclid, with Geometrical Exercises. By
J. EDWARDS, M.A., Second Master of King's College School.
Cheaper Edition. 2*s*.

Popular Poems, Selected by E. PARKER. Cheaper
Edition. 2*s*. 6*d*.

Readings in Poetry. Cheaper Edition. 3*s*. 6*d*.

Readings from Shakspeare. Edited by the Author
of "Aids to Development." 4*s*. 6*d*.

Readings in Prose. 4*s*. 6*d*.

Readings in Biography. 4*s*. 6*d*.

Readings in Science. 5*s*.

Class Reading Book. By G. LUDLOW, of Christ's
Hospital. 3*s*.

Abbott's Reader. Familiar Pieces in Prose and Verse.
By the Author of the "Young Christian." 3*s*.

Practical Introduction to English Composition.
By J. EDWARDS, M.A., of King's College. 2*s*.

Useful Arts employed in the Production of Food.
2*s*. 6*d*.

Useful Arts employed in the Production of Clothing.
2*s*. 6*d*.

Useful Arts employed in the Construction of Dwelling
Houses. 2*s*. 6*d*.

Le Tellier's French Grammar, practically adapted for English Teaching. By J. F. WATTEZ, one of the French Masters, King's College, London. 4s.

Ventouillac's Rudiments of the French Language; or, First French Reading-Book. Edited by J. F. WATTEZ. 3s. 6d.

Colloquial Exercises on the most Familiar Idioms of the French Language. By J. F. WATTEZ. 2s. 6d.

Practical Exercises on French Phraseology. By PROFESSOR BRASSEUR, of King's College. 3s. 6d.

Livre de Classe; with English Notes. By the late PROFESSOR VENTOUILLAC, of King's College. 5s.

French Poetry; with Notes by the same. 2s.

French Classics; abridged in a new form; and graciously permitted by Her Majesty to be used as Educational Works for the Instruction of the Royal Children of England. By MARIN DE LA VOYE, late French Master at Addiscombe.

Télémaque. 2s. 6d.	Pierre le Grand. 2s.
Voyages de Cyrus. 2s.	Charles XII. 2s.
Bélisaire. 1s. 6d.	Gil Blas. 4s.

By PROFESSOR BERNAYS, of King's College, London.

German Word Book: a Comparative Vocabulary displaying the affinity between the German and English Languages; with the Alphabet, Rules and Examples for Pronunciation. 3s.

German Phrase-Book; a Guide to the Formation of Sentences for Conversation and Composition. 3s.

German Grammar. 5s.

German Exercises. 5s. 6d.

German Examples, forming a Key to the Exercises. 3s.

German Reader, with Translations and Notes. 5s.

German Historical Anthology. 5s.

German Poetical Anthology. 7s.

Schiller's Maid of Orleans. With Notes. 2s.

Schiller's William Tell. With Notes. 2s.

Latin Grammar for Ladies. By R. W. BROWNE, M.A., Professor of Classical Literature in King's College, London. 1s. 6d.

Complete Latin Grammar for Learners. By J. W. DONALDSON, D.D., Head Master of King Edward's School, Bury St. Edmunds. 3s. 6d.

Exercises adapted to the Complete Latin Grammar. By Dr. DONALDSON. 2s. 6d.

Latin Exercises for the Junior Classes of King's College School. By the Rev. Dr. MAJOR, Head-Master. 2s. 6d.

Latin Exercises for Middle Forms in Schools. By the Rev. J. EDWARDS, M.A., Second Master of King's College School. 4s.

Rules and Exercises in the Use of the Latin Sub- junctive Mode. By the Rev. J. CROCKER, M.A. 4s.

Progressive Exercises for advanced Students in Latin Composition. Prepared for the Use of King's College, London, by the Rev. H. DAVIS. 3s. 6d.

Progressive Exercises in Latin Lyrics. By the Rev. J. EDWARDS. 3s.

Key to the Exercises in Lyrics. 2s. 6d.

Progressive Exercises in Latin Elegiacs and Heroics. By the same. 3s.

Catiline and Jugurtha of Sallust; with ANTHON'S Notes. Edited by the same. 2s. 6d. each.

Select Orations of Cicero, with English Notes. By a Master of King's College School, London. 2s. 6d.

Select Epistles of Cicero and Pliny. With English Notes. By the Rev. J. EDWARDS. 4s.

Æneid of Virgil, with ANTHON'S Notes. Edited by J. R. MAJOR, D.D., Head Master of King's College School. 7s. 6d.

C. Cornelii Taciti Opera ad Codices Antiquissimos, Commentario Critico. Edidit FRANCISCUS RITTER, Professor Bonnensis. Complete in Four Volumes. Octavo. 28s.

Aulularia and Menæchmei of Plautus, with Notes by JAMES HILDYARD, B.D., Fellow of Christ's College, Cambridge. 7s. 6d. each.

Græcæ Grammaticæ Rudimenta. Constructionis
Græcæ Præcepta; editio altera, cui præfixa est legitima decli-
nandi conjugandique ratio. 2*s.* 6*d.*

Also, strongly bound, 4*s.* 6*d.*

Complete Greek Grammar for Learners, by JOHN
W. DONALDSON, D.D., Head Master of King Edward's School,
Bury St. Edmund's.

First Greek Reader, from the German of JACOBS, with
English Notes. By the Rev. J. EDWARDS, M.A., of King's
College, London. Fourth and Cheaper Edition. 4*s.*

Excerpta ex Herodoto; with English Notes. By
Dr. MAJOR, Head Master of King's College School. 4*s.* 6*d.*

Excerpta ex Xenophontis Cyropædia; with a Vocabulary and Notes. By the same. 3*s.* 6*d.*

Xenophon's Anabasis of Cyrus. I. and II. With
English Notes, and Biographical Sketch, by Dr. HICKIE, Head
Master of Hawkeshead Grammar School. 3*s.* 6*d.*

Homer's Iliad. Books I. to III. With ANTHON'S
Notes, and Glossary. Edited by Dr. MAJOR. 6*s.*

Cambridge Greek and English Testament, printed in
parallel columns on the same page. Edited, for the Syndics of
the University Press, by Professor SCHOLEFIELD. 7*s.* 6*d.*

Cambridge Greek Testament. Strongly bound, 3*s.* 6*d.*

The Greek Text of the Acts of the Apostles. With
English Notes. By H. ROBINSON, D.D. 8*s.*

Selections from the Greek Verses of Shrewsbury
School; with an Account of the Iambic Metre and Style of Greek
Tragedy, and Exercises in Greek Tragic Senarii. By B. H.
KENNEDY, D.D., Head Master of Shrewsbury School. 8*s.*

Select Private Orations of Demosthenes. With English Notes. By the Rev. C. T. PENROSE, M.A., Head Master of
Sherborne School. 5*s.*

Frogs of Aristophanes. With English Notes. By
Rev. H. P. COOKESLEY. 7*s.*

Becker's Gallus; or, Roman Scenes of the Time of
Augustus. With Notes and Excursuses illustrative of the Man-
ners and Customs of the Romans. Translated by F. METCALFE,
M.A., Fellow of Lincoln College, Oxford. 12s.

Becker's Charicles; or, Illustrations of the Private
Life of the Greeks. Translated by F. METCALFE, M.A. 12s.

Student's Manual of Ancient History : Political History, Geographical Position, and Social State of the Principal
Nations of Antiquity. By W. C. TAYLOR, LL.D. 10s. 6d.

Student's Manual of Modern History : Rise and Pro-
gress of the Principal European Nations, their Political History,
and the Changes in their Social Condition. By W. C. TAYLOR,
LL.D. 10s. 6d.

Travels in the Track of the Ten Thousand Greeks; a
Geographical and Descriptive Account of the Expedition of
Cyrus, and of the Retreat of the Ten Thousand, as related by
Xenophon. By W. F. AINSWORTH, F.G.S. 7s. 6d.

Neander's Julian the Apostate and his Generation:
an Historical Picture. Translated by G. V. Cox, M.A. 3s. 6d.

Classical Examination Papers of King's College,
London. By R. W. BROWNE, M.A., Professor of Classical
Literature in King's College. 6s.

Aristophanis Comœdiæ Vndecim, cum Notis et Indice
Historice. Edidit HVBERTVS A. HOLDEN, A.M., Coll. Trin.
Cant. Socius ac Tutor. Octavo. 15s.

Dahlmann's Life of Herodotus drawn out from his
Book. Translated, with Notes, by G. V. Cox, M.A. 5s.

Life of Aristotle, including a Critical Discussion of
some Questions of Literary History connected with his Works.
By J. W. BLAKESLEY, B.D., late Fellow and Tutor of Trinity
College, Cambridge. 8s. 6d.

Schleiermacher's Introductions to the Dialogues of
Plato. Translated by the Rev. W. DODSON, M.A., Fellow of
Trinity College, Cambridge. 12s. 6d.

Fables of Babrius; with the Fragments of the lost
Fables. Edited by G. CORNEWALL LEWIS, M.A. 5s. 6d.

Pindar's Odes, revised and explained; with copious Notes and Indices. By J. W. DONALDSON, D.D., Head Master of Bury School. 16*s.*

Bœckh's Public Economy of Athens. Translated by G. C. LEWIS, A.M., late Student of Christ Church. Octavo. 18*s.*

Speeches of Demosthenes against Aphobus and Onetor. Translated, with Explanatory Notes, by C. R. KENNEDY, M.A., Fellow of Trinity College, Cambridge. 9*s.*

Stemmata Atheniensia; Tables of Biography, Chronology, and History, to facilitate the Study of the Classics. 5*s.*

Homeric Ballads: the Greek Text, with a Metrical Translation and Notes. By the late Dr. MAGINN. 6*s.*

CLASSICAL TEXTS,

Carefully Revised, from the best Editions.

Cicero de Senectute. 1*s.*

Cicero de Amicitia. 1*s.*

Cicero de Officiis. 2*s.*

Cicero pro Plancio. 1*s.*

Cicero pro Milone. 1*s.*

Cicero pro Muræna. 1*s.*

Ciceronis Oratio Philippica Secunda. 1*s.*

Taciti Germania. 1*s.*

Taciti Agricola. 1*s.*

Excerpta ex Taciti Annalibus. 2*s.* 6*d.*

Cæsar de Bello Gallico. I. to IV. 1*s.* 6*d.*

Virgilii Georgica. 1*s.* 6*d.*

Ovidii Fasti. 2*s.*

Horatii Satiræ. 1*s.*

Horatii Carmina. 1*s.* 6*d.*

Horatii Ars Poetica. 6*d.*

Terentii Andria. 1*s.*

Terentii Adelphi. 1*s.*

Platonis Phædo. 2*s.*

Platonis Menexenus. 1*s.*

Platonis Phædrus. 1*s.* 6*d.*

Excerpta ex Arriano. 2*s.* 6*d.*

Sophoclis Philoctetes, with English Notes. 2*s.*

Sophocles Œdipus Tyrannus, with English Notes. 2*s.* 6*d.*

Euripidis Bacchæ. 1*s.*

Æschyli Eumenides. 1*s.*

Æschyli Prometheus Vinctus. 1*s.*

Plutarch's Lives of Solon, Pericles, and Philopœmen. 2*s.*

LONDON: JOHN W. PARKER AND SON, WEST STRAND.

Lightning Source UK Ltd.
Milton Keynes UK
UKHW020647241218
334505UK00007B/123/P